S0-BFB-587

CONCEPTS AND CHALLENGES

EARTH'S STRUCTURE AND HISTORY

Leonard Bernstein ◆ Martin Schachter ◆ Alan Winkler ◆ Stanley Wolfe

Stanley Wolfe
Project Coordinator

GLOBE FEARON
Pearson Learning Group

The following people have contributed to the development of this product:

Art and Design: Evelyn Bauer, Susan Brorein, Tracey Gerber, Bernadette Hruby, Carol Marie Kiernan, Mindy Klarman, Judy Mahoney, Karen Mancinelli, Elbaliz Mendez, April Okano, Dan Thomas, Jennifer Visco

Editorial: Stephanie P. Cahill, Gina Dalessio, Nija Dixon, Martha Feehan, Theresa McCarthy, Maurice Sabean, Marilyn Sarch, Maury Solomon, Jeffrey Wickersty, Shirley C. White, S. Adrienn Vegh-Soti

Manufacturing: Mark Cirillo, Tom Dunne

Marketing: Douglas Falk, Maureen Christensen

Production: Irene Belinsky, Linda Bierniak, Carlos Blas, Karen Edmonds, Cheryl Golding, Leslie Greenberg, Roxanne Knoll, Susan Levine, Cynthia Lynch, Jennifer Murphy, Lisa Svoronos, Susan Tamm

Publishing Operations: Carolyn Coyle, Thomas Daning, Richetta Lobban

Technology: Jessie Lin, Ellen Strain, Joanne Saito

About the Cover: Earth's hard shell is formed from rocks and minerals. Salt is a mineral. The valley containing the salt flat shown in the larger photograph took millions of years to form. Scientists use fossils to study the history of Earth's structure and climate, and the history of the organisms living on it. The smaller photograph shows a fern fossil embedded in sedimentary rock.

Copyright © 2004 by Pearson Education, Inc., publishing as Globe Fearon®, an imprint of Pearson Learning Group, 299 Jefferson Road, Parsippany, NJ 07054. All rights reserved. No part of this book may be reproduced or transmitted in any form or by any means, electronic or mechanical, including photocopying, recording, or by any information storage and retrieval system, without permission in writing from the publisher. For information regarding permission(s), write to Rights and Permissions Department.

Globe Fearon® is a registered trademark of Globe Fearon, Inc.

ISBN: 0-13-024198-9

Printed in the United States of America

1 2 3 4 5 6 7 8 9 10   06 05 04 03

Globe Fearon
Pearson Learning Group

1-800-321-3106
www.pearsonlearning.com

Acknowledgments

Science Consultants

Gregory L. Vogt, Ed.D.
Associate Professor
Colorado State University
Fort Collins, CO

Stephen T. Lofthouse
Pace University
New York, NY

Laboratory Consultants

Sean M. Devine
Science Teacher
Ridge High School
Basking Ridge, NJ

Vincent R. Dionisio
Science Teacher
Clifton High School
Clifton, NJ

Reading Consultant

Sharon Cook
Consultant
Leadership in Literacy

Internet Consultant

Janet M. Gaudino
Science Teacher
Montgomery Middle School
Skillman, NJ

ESL/ELL Consultant

Elizabeth Jimenez
Consultant
Pomona, CA

Content Reviewers

Marian B. Jacobs Ph.D. (Chs. 1, 2, 3, 4)
Columbia University
New York, NY

Terry Moran (pp. 30–31)
Moran Research Service
Harvard, MA

Todd Woerner (pp. 84–85)
Department of Chemistry
Duke University
Durham, NC

Teacher Reviewers

Peggy L. Cook
Lakeworth Middle School
Lakeworth, FL

Claudia Toback
Consultant/Mentor
Staten Island, NY

Contents

Scientific Skills and Investigations Handbooks

Chapter 1 The Structure of Earth — 15

Chapter 2 Minerals and Their Properties — 41

Features

What are scientific skills?

People are naturally curious. They want to understand the world around them. They want to understand what causes earthquakes and where is the best place to search for useful minerals. The field of science would probably not exist if it were not for human curiosity about the natural world.

People also want to be able to make good guesses about the future. They want to be able to track severe storms such as hurricanes and to find ways to protect their homes against flooding.

Scientists use many skills to explore the world and gather information about it. These skills are called science process skills. Another name for them is science inquiry skills.

Science process skills allow you to think like a scientist. They help you identify problems and answer questions. Sometimes they help you solve problems. More often, they provide some possible answers and lead to more questions. In this book, you will use a variety of science process skills to understand the facts and theories in Earth science.

Science process skills are not only used in science. You compare prices when you shop and you observe what happens to foods when you cook them. You predict what the weather will be by looking at the sky. In fact, science process skills are really everyday life skills that have been adapted for problem solving in science.

▲ **Figure 1**
Scientists use science process skills to understand how gravity affects the way crystals grow and materials mix, how caves form and change, how the land is built up and then torn down, and what Earth's place is in the universe.

1 ▶ NAME: What is the name for the skills scientists use to solve problems?

Contents

1 Observing and Comparing

Making Observations An important part of solving any problem is observing, or using your senses to find out what is going on around you. The five senses are sight, hearing, touch, smell, and taste. When you look at a pebble and feel its smoothness, you are observing. When you observe, you pay close attention to everything that happens around you.

Scientists observe the world in ways that other scientists can repeat. This is a goal of scientific observation. It is expected that when a scientist has made an observation, other people will be able to make the same observation.

 LIST: What are the five senses?

Comparing and Contrasting Part of observing is comparing and contrasting. When you compare data, you observe the characteristics of several things or events to see how they are alike. When you contrast data, you look for ways that similar things are different from one another.

▲ **Figure 2** River and glacial cut valleys look similar. However, you can see many differences from the valley floor.

COMPARE/CONTRAST: How are valleys carved by running water and valleys carved by glaciers similar? How are they different?

Using Tools to Observe Sometimes an object is too small to see with your eyes alone. You need a special tool to help you make observations. One tool that scientists use to observe is the seismograph. A seismograph detects earthquakes by measuring the vibrations of Earth's crust.

▲ **Figure 3** Seismologist checking a seismograph

INFER: Besides detecting earthquakes, what other use does a seismograph have?

Hands-On Activity

MAKING OBSERVATIONS

You and a partner will need 2 shoeboxes with lids, 2 rubber bands, and several small objects.

1. Place several small objects into the shoebox. Do not let your partner see what you put into the shoebox.
2. Cover the shoebox with the lid. Put a rubber band around the shoebox to keep the lid on.
3. Exchange shoeboxes with your partner.
4. Gently shake, turn, and rattle the shoebox.
5. Try to describe what is in the shoebox without opening it. Write your descriptions on a sheet of paper.

Practicing Your Skills

6. **IDENTIFY:** What science process skill did you use?
7. **IDENTIFY:** Which of your senses was most important to you?
8. **ANALYZE:** Direct observation is seeing something with your eyes or hearing it with your ears. Indirect observation involves using a model or past experience to make a guess about something. Which kind of observation did you use?

2 Classifying Data

Key Term

data: information you collect when you observe something

Collecting and Classifying Data The information you collect when you observe something is called **data.** The data from an experiment or from observations you have made are first recorded, or written down. Then, they are classified.

When you classify data, you group things together based on how they are alike. This information often comes from making comparisons as you observe. You may classify by size, shape, color, use, or any other important feature. Classifying data helps you recognize and understand the relationships between things. Classification makes studying large groups of things easier. For example, Earth scientists use classification to organize the different types of rocks and minerals.

▶ 5 EXPLAIN: How can you classify data?

Hands-On Activity

ORGANIZING ROCKS

You will need 15 pebbles of different colors, textures, and shapes.

1. Lay the pebbles out on a table. Classify the pebbles into two categories based on texture: *Smooth* and *Rough.*

2. Look at the pebbles you classified as smooth. Divide these pebbles into new categories based on similar colors.

3. Repeat Step 2 for the pebbles you classified as rough.

Practicing Your Skills

4. ANALYZE: How did you classify the pebbles? What other ways could you classify the pebbles?

5. EXPLAIN: Why is a classification system useful?

3 Modeling and Simulating

Key Terms

model: tool scientists use to represent an object or process

simulation: computer model that usually shows a process

Modeling Sometimes things are too small to see with your eyes alone. Other times, an object is too large to see. You may need a model to help you examine the object. A **model** is a good way to show what a very small or a very large object looks like. A model can have more details than what may be seen with just your eyes. It can be used to represent a process or an object that is hard to explain with words. A model can be a three-dimensional picture, a drawing, a computer image, or a diagram.

▶ 6 DEFINE: What is a model?

Simulating A **simulation** is a kind of model that shows a process. It is often done using a computer. You can use a simulation to predict the outcome of an experiment. Scientists use simulations to study everything from the insides of a volcano to the development of a tornado.

▲ **Figure 4** This student is discovering how volcanoes are created through successive layers of erupted lava.

▶ 7 DEFINE: What is a simulation?

4 Measuring

Key Terms

unit: amount used to measure something

meter: basic unit of length or distance

mass: amount of matter in something

gram: basic unit of mass

volume: amount of space an object takes up

liter: basic unit of liquid volume

meniscus: curve at the surface of a liquid in a thin tube

temperature: measure of the amount of heat energy something contains

Two Systems of Measurement When you measure, you compare an unknown value with a known value using standard units. A **unit** is an amount used to measure something. The metric system is an international system of measurement. Examples of metric units are the gram, the kilometer, and the liter. In the United States, the English system and the metric system are both used. Examples of units in the English system are the pound, the foot, and the gallon.

There is also a more modern form of the metric system called SI. The letters *SI* stand for the French words *Système International.* Many of the units in the SI are the same as those in the metric system.

The metric and SI systems are both based on units of 10. This makes them easy to use. Each unit in these systems is ten times greater than the one before it. To show a change in the size of a unit, you add a prefix to the unit. The prefix tells you whether the unit is larger or smaller. For example, a centimeter is ten times bigger than a millimeter.

PREFIXES AND THEIR MEANINGS	
kilo-	one thousand (1,000)
hecto-	one hundred (100)
deca-	ten (10)
deci-	one-tenth (1/10)
centi-	one-hundredth (1/100)
milli-	one-thousandth (1/1,000)

◀ Figure 5

8 IDENTIFY: What are two measurement systems?

Units of Length Length is the distance from one point to another. In the metric system, the basic unit of length or distance is the **meter.** A meter is about the length from a doorknob to the floor. Longer distances, such as the distances between cities, are measured in kilometers. A kilometer is 1,000 meters. Centimeters and millimeters measure shorter distances. A centimeter is 1/100 of a meter. A millimeter is 1/1,000 of a meter. Figure 6 compares common units of length. It also shows the abbreviation for each unit.

SI/METRIC UNITS OF LENGTH	
1,000 millimeters (mm)	1 meter (m)
100 centimeters (cm)	1 meter
10 decimeters (dm)	1 meter
10 millimeters	1 centimeter
1,000 meters	1 kilometer (km)

▲ Figure 6

Length can be measured with a meter stick. A meter stick is 1 m long and is divided into 100 equal lengths by numbered lines. The distance between each of these lines is equal to 1 cm. Each centimeter is divided into ten equal parts. Each one of these parts is equal to 1 mm.

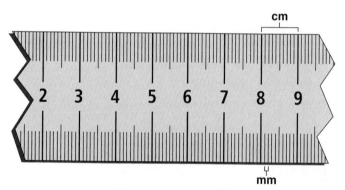

▲ Figure 7 A meter stick is divided into centimeters and millimeters.

9 CALCULATE: How many centimeters are there in 3 m?

Measuring Area Do you know how people find the area of the floor of a room? They measure the length and the width of the room. Then, they multiply the two numbers. You can find the area of any rectangle by multiplying its length by its width. Area is expressed in square units, such as square meters (m²) or square centimeters (cm²).

$$\text{Area} = \text{length} \times \text{width}$$

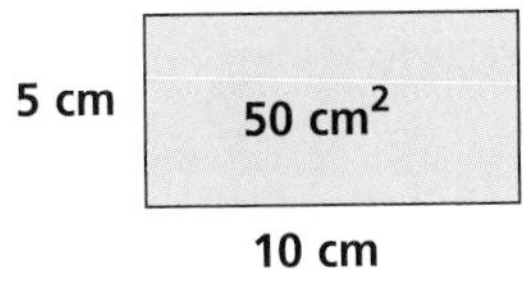

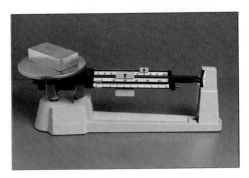

◀ **Figure 8** The area of a rectangle equals length times width.

5 cm | 50 cm² | 10 cm

10 CALCULATE: What is the area of a rectangle 2 cm × 3 cm?

Mass and Weight The amount of matter in something is its **mass.** The basic metric unit of mass is called a **gram (g).** A paper clip has about 1 g of mass. Mass is measured with an instrument called a balance. A balance works like a seesaw. It compares an unknown mass with a known mass.

One kind of balance that is commonly used to measure mass is a triple-beam balance. A triple-beam balance has a pan. The object being measured is placed on the pan. The balance also has three beams. Weights, called riders, are moved along each beam until the object on the pan is balanced. Each rider gives a reading in grams. The mass of the object is equal to the total readings of all three riders.

◀ **Figure 9**
A triple-beam balance

Mass and weight are related; however, they are not the same. The weight of an object is a measure of Earth's pull of gravity between Earth and that object. Gravity is the force that pulls objects toward the center of Earth. The strength of the pull of gravity between two objects depends on the distance between the objects and how much mass they each contain. So, the weight changes as its distance from the center of Earth changes.

11 IDENTIFY: What instrument is used to measure mass?

Volume The amount of space an object takes up is its **volume.** You can measure the volume of liquids and solids. Liquid volume is usually measured in **liters.** Soft drinks in the United States often come in 2-liter bottles.

A graduated cylinder is used to measure liquid volume. Graduated cylinders are calibrated, or marked off, at regular intervals. Look at Figure 10. It shows a graduated cylinder. On this graduated cylinder, each small line is equal to 0.05 mL. The longer lines mark off every 0.25 mL up to 5.00 mL. However, every graduated cylinder is not calibrated in this manner. They come in different sizes up to 2,000 mL, with different calibrations.

Always read the measurement at eye level. If you are using a glass graduated cylinder, you will need to read the mark on the graduated cylinder closest to the bottom of the meniscus. A **meniscus** is the curve at the surface of a liquid in a thin tube. A plastic graduated cylinder does not show a meniscus.

▲ **Figure 10** This glass graduated cylinder shows a meniscus.

The volume of solid objects is often measured in cubic centimeters. One cubic centimeter equals 1 milliliter (mL).

Look at Figure 11. Each side of the cube is 1 cm long. The volume of the cube is 1 cubic centimeter (cm^3). Now, look at the drawing of the box in Figure 12. Its length is 3 cm. Its width is 2 cm. Its height is 2 cm. The volume of the box can be found by multiplying length by width by height. In this case, volume equals $3 \times 2 \times 2$. Therefore, the volume of the box is 12 cm^3.

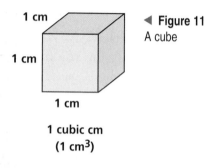

◀ **Figure 11**
A cube

1 cubic cm
(1 cm^3)

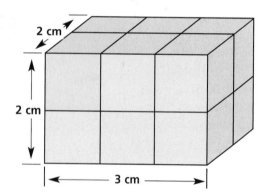

▲ **Figure 12** The volume of a box equals length by width by height.

$$V = L \times W \times H$$

If you have a box that is 10 cm on each side, its volume would be 1,000 cm^3. A liter is the same as 1,000 cm^3. One liter of liquid will fill the box exactly.

12▶ CALCULATE: How many milliliters of water would fill a 12-cm^3 box?

Hands-On Activity

CALCULATING AREA AND VOLUME

You will need 3 boxes of different sizes, paper, and a metric ruler.

1. Measure the length, width, and height of each box in centimeters. Record each measurement in your notes.

2. Calculate the volume of each box. Record each volume in your notes.

3. Find the surface area of each box. Record each area in your notes.

Practicing Your Skills

4. ANALYZE: Which of the three boxes has the largest volume?

5. CALCULATE: How many milliliters of liquid would fill each box?

6. ANALYZE: What is the surface area of the largest box?

Temperature **Temperature** is a measure of the amount of heat energy something contains. An instrument that measures temperature is called a thermometer.

Most thermometers are glass tubes. At the bottom of the tube is a wider part, called the bulb. The bulb is filled with liquid. Liquids that are often used include mercury, colored alcohol, or colored water. When heat is added, the liquid expands, or gets larger. It rises in the glass tube. When heat is taken away, the liquid contracts, or gets smaller. The liquid falls in the tube. On the side of the tube is a series of marks. You read the temperature by looking at the mark on the tube where the liquid stops.

Temperature can be measured on three different scales. These scales are the Fahrenheit (F) scale, the Celsius (C) scale, and the Kelvin (K) scale. The Fahrenheit scale is part of the English system of measurement. The Celsius scale is usually used in science. Almost all scientists, even in the United States, use the Celsius scale. Each unit on the Celsius scale is a degree Celsius (°C). The degree Celsius is the metric unit of temperature. Water freezes at 0°C. It boils at 100°C.

Scientists working with very low temperatures use the Kelvin scale. The Kelvin scale is part of the SI measurement system. It begins at absolute zero, or 0K. This number indicates, in theory at least, a total lack of heat.

COMPARING TEMPERATURE SCALES			
	Kelvin	Fahrenheit	Celsius
Boiling point of water	373K	212°F	100°C
Human body temperature	310K	98.6°F	37°C
Freezing point of water	273K	32°F	0°C
Absolute zero	0K	−459.67°F	−273.15°C

▲ Figure 13

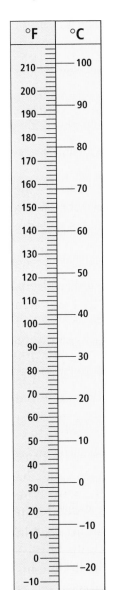

◄ Figure 14 The Fahrenheit and Celsius scales

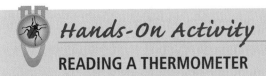

Hands-On Activity

READING A THERMOMETER

You will need safety goggles, a lab apron, 2 beakers, a heat source, ice water, a wax pencil, a ruler, and a standard Celsius thermometer.

1. Boil some water in a beaker.
   ⚠CAUTION: Be very careful when working with heat. Place your thermometer in the beaker. Do not let the thermometer touch the sides or bottom of the beaker. Wait until the mercury rises as far as it will go. Record the temperature.

2. Fill a beaker with ice water. Place the unmarked thermometer into this beaker. Wait until the mercury goes as low as it will go. Record the temperature.

▲ STEP 1 Record the temperature of the boiling water.

Practicing Your Skills

3. IDENTIFY: What is the temperature at which the mercury rose as high as it would go?

4. IDENTIFY: What is the temperature at which the mercury went as low as it would go?

13▶ NAME: What are the three scales used to measure temperature?

5 Analyzing Data and Communicating Results

Key Term

communication: sharing information

Analyzing Data When you organize information, you put it in a logical order. In scientific experiments, it is important to organize your data. Data collected during an experiment are not very useful unless they are organized and easy to read. It is also important to organize your data if you plan to share the results of your experiment.

Scientists often organize information visually by using data tables, charts, graphs, and diagrams. By using tables, charts, graphs, and diagrams, scientists can display a lot of information in a small space. They also make it easier to compare and interpret data.

Tables are made up of rows and columns. Columns run up and down. Rows run from left to right. Tables usually show numerical data. Information in the table can be arranged in time order. It can also be set up to show patterns or trends. A table showing wind speed can reveal the effects the speed of wind will have on land. Figure 15 shows a table of gases in the atmosphere.

GASES IN THE ATMOSPHERE	
Gas	Percentage
Oxygen	21
Carbon dioxide	0.04
Nitrogen	78
Water vapor, helium, and other gases	0.02
Argon	0.94

▲ Figure 15

Graphs, such as bar graphs, line graphs, and circle graphs, often use special coloring, shading, or patterns to represent information. Keys indicate what the special markings represent. Line graphs have horizontal (x) and vertical (y) axes to indicate such things as time and quantities.

14 ▶ EXPLAIN: How do tables and graphs help you analyze data?

Sharing Results When you talk to a friend, you are communicating, or sharing information. If you write a letter or a report, you are also communicating but in a different way. Scientists communicate all the time. They communicate to share results, information, and opinions. They write books and magazine or newspaper articles. They may also create Web sites about their work. This is called written **communication.**

Graphs are a visual way to communicate. The circle graph in Figure 16 is showing the same information from Figure 15. The circle graph presents the information in a different way.

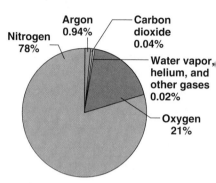

▲ **Figure 16** Circle graphs are a good way to show parts of a whole.

15 ▶ LIST: What are some ways to communicate the results of an experiment?

6 Making Predictions

Key Terms

infer: to form a conclusion

predict: to state ahead of time what you think is going to happen

Thinking of Possibilities When you **infer** something, you form a conclusion. This is called making an inference. Your conclusion will usually be based on observations or past experience. You may use logic to form your statement. Your statement might be supported by evidence and perhaps can be tested by an experiment. An inference is not a fact. It is only one possible explanation.

When you **predict,** you state ahead of time what you think will happen. Predictions about future events are based on inferences, evidence, or past experience. The two science process skills of inferring and predicting are very closely related.

16 ▶ CONTRAST: What is the difference between inferring and predicting?

How do you conduct a scientific investigation?

By now, you should have a good understanding of the science process skills. These skills are used to solve many science problems. There is also a basic procedure, or plan, that scientists usually follow when conducting investigations. Some people call this procedure the scientific method.

The scientific method is a series of steps that can serve as a guide to solving problems or answering questions. It uses many of the science process skills you know, such as observing and predicting.

Not all experiments use all of the steps in the scientific method. Some experiments follow all of them, but in a different order. In fact, there is no one right scientific method. Each problem is different. Some problems may require steps that another problem would not. However, most investigations will follow the same basic procedure.

1 ▶ DESCRIBE: What is the scientific method?

▲ **Figure 1** Scientists use the scientific method to guide experiments.

Contents

1 Identifying a Problem and Doing Research

Starting an Investigation Scientists often state a problem as a question. This is the first step in a scientific investigation. Most experiments begin by asking a scientific question. That is, they ask a question that can be answered by gathering evidence. This question is the reason for the scientific investigation. It also helps determine how the investigation will proceed.

Have you ever done background research for a science project? When you do this kind of research, you are looking for data that others have already obtained on the same subject. You can gather research by reading books, magazines, and newspapers, and by using the Internet to find out what other scientists have done. Doing research is the first step of gathering evidence for a scientific investigation.

 IDENTIFY: What is the first step of a scientific investigation?

BUILDING SCIENCE SKILLS

Researching Background Information Suppose you notice that a river running through your town looks brown on some days and clear on others. You also notice that when the river turns brown, it has usually rained the day before. You wonder if rain and the brown color of the river water are related.

To determine if the river water color is related to rainfall, look for information on rivers in encyclopedias, in geology books, and on the Internet. Put your findings in a report.

▲ **Figure 2** Water in river after a heavy rain.

2 Forming a Hypothesis

Key Terms

hypothesis: suggested answer to a question or problem

theory: set of hypotheses that have been supported by testing over and over again

Focusing the Investigation Scientists usually state clearly what they expect to find out in an investigation. This is called stating a hypothesis. A **hypothesis** is a suggested answer to a question or a solution to a problem. Stating a hypothesis helps to keep you focused on the problem and helps you decide what to test.

To form their hypotheses, scientists must think of possible explanations for a set of observations or they must suggest possible answers to a scientific question. One of those explanations becomes the hypothesis. In science, a hypothesis must include something that can be tested.

A hypothesis is more than just a guess. It must consider observations, past experiences, and previous knowledge. It is an inference turned into a statement that can be tested. A set of hypotheses that have been supported by testing over and over again by many scientists is called a **theory.** An example is the theory that explains how living things have evolved, or changed, over time.

A hypothesis can take the form of an "if…then" statement. A well-worded hypothesis is a guide for how to set up and perform an experiment.

 DESCRIBE: How does a scientist form a hypothesis?

BUILDING SCIENCE SKILLS

Developing a Hypothesis If you are testing how river water and rainfall are related, you might write down this hypothesis:

Runoff is one cause of the river water turning brown.

Your hypothesis is incomplete. It is not enough to link water color and rainfall. You need to explain what materials make the river water brown and how rainfall causes those materials to get into the water. Revise the hypothesis above to make it more specific.

3 Designing and Carrying Out an Experiment

Key Terms

variable: anything that can affect the outcome of an experiment

constant: something that does not change

controlled experiment: experiment in which all the conditions except one are kept constant

Testing the Hypothesis Scientists need to plan how to test their hypotheses. This means they must design an experiment. The plan must be a step-by-step procedure. It should include a record of any observations made or measurements taken.

All experiments must take variables into account. A **variable** is anything that can affect the outcome of an experiment. Room temperature, amount of sunlight, and water vapor in the air are just some of the many variables that could affect the outcome of an experiment.

4 ▶ DEFINE: What is a variable?

Controlling the Experiment One of the variables in an experiment should be what you are testing. This is what you will change during the experiment. All other variables need to remain the same. In this experiment, you will vary the type of earth.

A **constant** is something that does not change. If there are no constants in your experiment, you will not be sure why you got the results you did. An experiment in which all the conditions except one are kept constant is called a **controlled experiment.**

Some experiments have two setups. In one setup, called the control, nothing is changed. In the other setup, the variable being tested is changed. Later, the control group can be compared with the other group to provide useful data.

5 ▶ EXPLAIN: Explain how a controlled experiment is set up.

Designing the Procedure Suppose you now want to design an experiment to determine what makes river water brown. You have your hypothesis. You decide your procedure is to construct a slightly tilted model of the river, the town, and the land upstream from the town. You will send water down the river and measure the color and clarity of the water. Next, you will create artificial rain and again check the color and clarity of the water.

Does it matter how much rain you add to your model? Does it matter how heavy the rainfall is? Does 3 inches (7.5 cm) of rainfall in 5 minutes have the same effect on your model as 3 inches in 1 hour?

In designing your experiment, you need to identify the variables. The amount of water and the rate at which you apply it to your model are variables that could affect the outcome of your experiment. Another important variable for your experiment is the steepness of the river. To be sure of your results, you will have to conduct your experiment several times. Each time you will alter just one variable while keeping the other variables just the same.

Finally, you should decide on the data you will collect. How will you measure the color and clarity of the water of the river? You might make a color chart that you lower into the river water to see how the sediment in the water changes its color.

The hands-on activity on page 12 is an example of an experiment you might have designed.

◀ **Figure 3** In your experiment, you will elevate the trays with books to test soil runoff.

6 ▶ EXPLAIN: How do constants and variables affect an experiment?

Hands-On Activity

CARRYING OUT AN EXPERIMENT

You will need 2 styrofoam meat trays from the grocery store, garden soil, grass sod, 2 plastic drinking glasses, 2 books, sprinkling can, scissors, and water. You should wear an apron and safety goggles.

1. Cut a small drain notch from the center of one end of each tray.
   ⚠ CAUTION: Be careful when using scissors.

2. Fill one tray with about a 1-inch layer (2.5 cm) of garden soil. Leave 2 inches (5 cm) of the notched end of the tray empty of soil.

3. Fill the second tray with a layer of sod except for 2 inches at the end with the notch.

4. Place the notched end of each tray at the edge of a table so that the trays extend over the edge a short distance.

5. Elevate the other end of the trays with books.

6. Label the cups Soil and Sod.

7. Sprinkle the soil tray with water. Keep sprinkling until the water runs off the surface of the soil and pours out the notch drain. Collect a glass of runoff water.

8. Repeat Step 7 with the sod tray.

Practicing Your Skills

9. OBSERVE: How much water did you have to sprinkle on the soil tray in order to collect a full glass?

10. OBSERVE: How much water did you have to sprinkle on the sod tray in order to collect a full glass?

11. COMPARE: Which glass had the dirtiest water?

12. EXPLAIN: What caused the difference in water clarity in the two cups?

13. INFER: What would be the best way to reduce soil runoff in rivers?

4 Recording and Analyzing Data

Dealing With Data During an experiment, you must keep careful notes about what you observe. For example, you might need to note how long the rain fell on the trays before water began running off. How fast did the water run off each tray? This is important information that might affect your conclusion.

At the end of an experiment, you will need to study the data to find any patterns. Much of the data you will deal with is written text such as a report or a summary of an experiment. However, scientific information is often a set of numbers or facts presented in other, more visual ways. These visual presentations make the information easier to understand. Tables, charts, and graphs, for instance, help you understand a collection of facts on a topic.

After your data have been organized, you need to ask what the data show. Do they support your hypothesis? Do they show something wrong in your experiment? Do you need to gather more data by performing another experiment?

 LIST: What are some ways to display data?

BUILDING SCIENCE SKILLS

Analyzing Data You made the following notes during your experiment. How would you display this information?

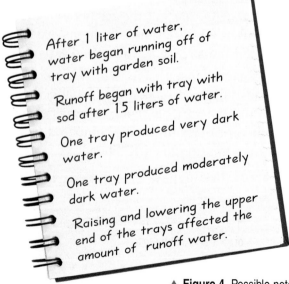

▲ **Figure 4** Possible notes

5 Stating a Conclusion

Drawing Conclusions A conclusion is a statement that sums up what you have learned from an experiment. When you draw a conclusion, you need to decide whether the data you collected supported your hypothesis. You may need to repeat an experiment several times before you can draw any conclusions from it. Conclusions often lead you to ask new questions and plan new experiments to answer them.

8 EXPLAIN: Why might it be necessary to repeat an experiment?

BUILDING SCIENCE SKILLS

Stating a Conclusion Review your hypothesis statement regarding the effect of surface material on rainwater runoff. Then, review the data you obtained during the experiment.

- Was your hypothesis correct? Use your observations to support your answer.
- Which surface reduced soil runoff better?

▲ **Figure 5** Throughout this program, you may use forms like these to organize your lab reports.

6 Writing a Report

Communicating Results Scientists keep careful written records of their observations and findings. These records are used to create a lab report. Lab reports are a form of written communication. They explain what happened in the experiment. A good lab report should be written so that anyone reading it can duplicate the experiment. It should contain the following information:

- A title
- A purpose
- Background information
- Your hypothesis
- Materials used
- Your step-by-step procedure
- Your observations
- Your recorded data
- Your analysis of the data
- Your conclusions

Your conclusions should relate back to the questions you asked in the "purpose" section of your report. Also, the report should not have any experimental errors that might have caused unexpected results. For example, did you follow the steps in the correct order? Did an unexpected variable interfere with your results? Was your equipment clean and in good working order? This explanation of possible errors should also be part of your conclusions.

9 EXPLAIN: Why is it important to explain possible errors in your lab report?

BUILDING SCIENCE SKILLS

Writing a Lab Report Write a lab report to communicate to other scientists your discoveries about soil runoff. Your lab report should include a title, your hypothesis statement, a list of materials you used, the procedure, your observations, and your conclusions. Try to include one table of data in your report.

LAB SAFETY

Working in a science laboratory can be both exciting and meaningful. However, you must always be aware of safety precautions when carrying out experiments. There are a few basic rules that should be followed in any science laboratory:

- Read all instructions carefully before the start of an experiment. Follow all instructions exactly and in the correct order.

- Check your equipment to make sure it is clean and working properly.

- Never taste, smell, or touch any substance in the lab that you are not told to do so. Never eat or drink anything in the lab. Do not chew gum.

- Never work alone. Tell a teacher at once if an accident occurs.

Experiments that use chemicals or heat can be dangerous. The following list of rules and symbols will help you avoid accidents. There are also rules about what to do if an accident does occur. Here are some rules to remember when working in a lab:

 1. Do not use glass that is chipped or metal objects with broken edges. Do not try to clean up broken glassware yourself. Notify your teacher if a piece of glassware is broken.

 2. Do not use electrical cords with loose plugs or frayed ends. Do not let electrical cords cross in front of working areas. Do not use electrical equipment near water.

 3. Be very careful when using sharp objects such as scissors, knives, or tweezers. Always cut in a direction away from your body.

 4. Be careful when you are using a heat source. Use proper equipment, such as tongs or a ringstand, when handling hot objects.

 5. Confine loose clothing and hair when working with an open flame. Be sure you know the location of the nearest fire extinguisher. Never reach across an open flame.

 6. Be careful when working with poisonous or toxic substances. Never mix chemicals without directions from your teacher. Remove any long jewelry that might hang down and end up in chemicals. Avoid touching your eyes or mouth when working with chemicals.

 7. Use extreme care when working with acids and bases. Never mix acids and bases without direction from your teacher. Never smell anything directly. Use caution when handling chemicals that produce fumes.

 8. Wear safety goggles, especially when working with an open flame, chemicals, and any liquids.

 9. Wear lab aprons when working with substances of any sort, especially chemicals.

 10. Use caution when handling or collecting plants. Some plants can be harmful if they are touched or eaten.

 11. Use caution when handling live animals. Some animals can injure you or spread disease. Handle all live animals as humanely as possible.

 12. Dispose of all equipment and materials properly. Keep your work area clean at all times.

 13. Always wash your hands thoroughly with soap and water after handling chemicals or live organisms.

 14. Follow the ⚠ CAUTION and safety symbols you see used throughout this book when doing labs or other activities.

Chapter 1 The Structure of Earth

▲ **Figure 1-1** Earth as seen from space

This is an image of Earth created by an artificial satellite in space. Artificial satellites are sent into orbit for many purposes. For example, some satellites are used to study our planet and other objects in space. They help us to map Earth's surface and determine the size and shape of Earth. They also are used to study the land, oceans, and air. Computers can be used to reveal even more detail.

▶The satellite image in Figure 1-1 shows some physical features of Earth. Which ones can you identify?

Contents

1-1 How do scientists study Earth?

1-1

Objective

Identify and describe the ways scientists study Earth.

Key Terms

Earth science: study of Earth and its history

specialist (SPEHSH-uhl-ihst)**:** person who studies or works on only one part of a subject

Studying Earth Science is an organized collection of knowledge about everything in the universe. The scientific study of Earth and its history is called **Earth science.** Some scientists study the rocks and soil that make up parts of Earth. Other scientists study how Earth is part of the solar system.

Earth is much more than rocks and soils. When seen from space, the more obvious features are the clouds and oceans. To study Earth, scientists do not just look at land, water, and air. They must study how land, air, and water interact.

Earth science is like a jigsaw puzzle made up of four pieces. Each piece of the puzzle is a main branch of Earth science. The four main branches of Earth science are geology, oceanography, meteorology, and astronomy. Together, they make up the field of Earth science. Look at Figure 1-2 below to learn something about each of the four main branches.

▶ 1 IDENTIFY: What are the four main branches of Earth science?

Specialists in Earth Science A **specialist** is a person who studies or works on only one part of a subject. This one part of the subject is called a specialty.

There are many Earth science specialties. Most Earth scientists are specialists. For example, some oceanographers study only waves and tides. Others study the makeup of ocean water. Still others study the ocean bottom or deep-sea vents.

▶ 2 DESCRIBE: What is meant by a specialty?

BRANCHES OF EARTH SCIENCE

Geology
Geologists study the forces that shape Earth. Some careers in geology are mineralogist, volcanologist, and soil conservationist.

Oceanography
Oceanographers study Earth's oceans. Underwater photographer and marine biologist are just two of the many careers in oceanography.

Meteorology
Meteorologists gather information from around the world about conditions in the atmosphere. Some careers in meteorology are weather observer and weather forecaster.

Astronomy
Astronomers study the universe beyond Earth. Rocket scientist and astronaut are careers in this field.

▲ Figure 1-2

The Importance of Earth Science Earth science is an important part of our everyday lives. The observations and discoveries made by Earth scientists affect us in many ways.

For example, weather information is collected by Earth scientists called meteorologists. Meteorologists are able to give early warnings about severe storms such as hurricanes and tornadoes. Storm warnings can help save lives and limit property damage. Geologists help locate oil and coal supplies. These fuels are used to heat homes, run cars, and generate electricity. Oceanographers study the ocean and map currents. These help in containing oil spills and the cleaning of polluted waters.

Exploring space and experiments done in space have led to new medicines and technologies. They have also led to improvements in radios, televisions, and telephones. The development of the space shuttle led to improvements in fire-resistant materials.

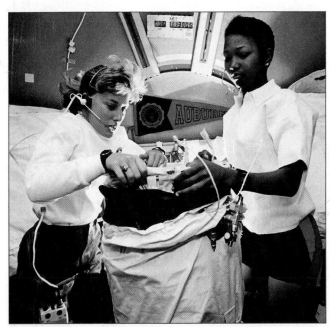

▲ **Figure 1-3** Astronauts carry out Earth science experiments in space that help us on Earth.

▶ **EXPLAIN:** Why is the study of weather important to our lives every day?

☑ CHECKING CONCEPTS

1. The study of Earth and how it changes is called _____.

2. A mineralogist studies the branch of Earth science called _____.

3. The study of Earth's oceans is called _____.

4. The study of space is part of the branch of Earth science called _____.

5. Another name for a weather forecaster is a _____.

💡 THINKING CRITICALLY

6. **CLASSIFY:** In which field of Earth science would you study each of these subjects?
   a. coral reefs   d. the planet Jupiter
   b. the Grand Canyon   e. soil quality
   c. hurricanes

7. **ANALYZE:** What is one way, other than weather, in which the study of Earth science affected you today?

Web InfoSearch

Earth Science Careers Choose an Earth science career from the ones that are mentioned in Figure 1-2 or another one that you have heard about.

SEARCH: Use the Internet to find out more information about the career you chose. How much education is required? What tools are generally used on the job? What is the average salary for a person who has some experience? What fields of study in this career would interest you most? What on-the-job activities would you enjoy most? Start your search at www.conceptsandchallenges.com. Some key search words are **Earth science careers, meteorology, geology, oceanography,** and **astronomy.**

◀ **Figure 1-4** As a geologist, you might study rock formations like this one.

What are the main parts of Earth?

Objective

Name and describe the three main parts of Earth: the lithosphere, hydrosphere, and atmosphere.

Key Terms

sphere (SFEER): round, three-dimensional object

lithosphere (LIHTH-oh-sfeer): solid part of Earth

hydrosphere (HY-droh-sfeer): part of Earth that is water

atmosphere (AT-muhs-feer): envelope of gases surrounding Earth

The Lithosphere   A **sphere** is a round, three-dimensional object. Earth is spherical in shape. The prefix *litho-* means "stone." The solid part of Earth is called the **lithosphere.** The ground you walk on is part of the lithosphere. Mountains are raised parts of the lithosphere. Valleys, found between mountains, are low areas of the lithosphere.

The lithosphere includes the continents as well as the land under the oceans. Continents are very large landmasses. The seven continents found on Earth today are shown in Figure 1-5.

▶ **1 NAME:** What is the solid part of Earth called?

The Hydrosphere   The part of Earth that is water is called the **hydrosphere.** The hydrosphere includes all of the liquid water and ice on Earth. Salt water makes up about 97 percent of Earth's water. Most of the salt water is found in the oceans. There are three major oceans on Earth: Atlantic, Pacific, and Indian. These are all interconnected to form one large world ocean. The remaining 3 percent is fresh water. Fresh water is found mostly in rivers, lakes, glaciers, and the polar ice caps.

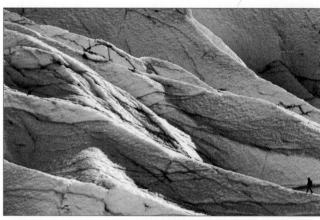

▲ **Figure 1-6** Much of the fresh water on Earth is found frozen in glaciers. This glacier is in Alaska.

▶ **2 NAME:** List the bodies of salt water that are shown in Figure 1-5.

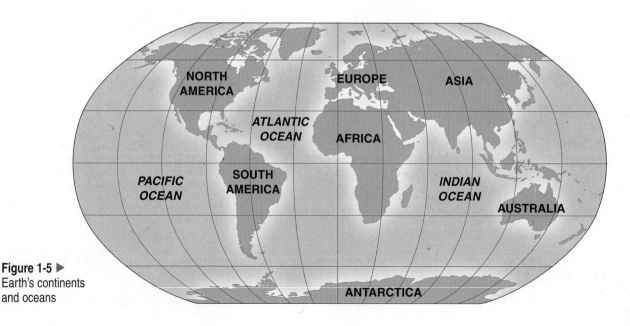

Figure 1-5 ▶
Earth's continents and oceans

NORTH AMERICA

EUROPE

ASIA

ATLANTIC OCEAN

AFRICA

PACIFIC OCEAN

SOUTH AMERICA

INDIAN OCEAN

AUSTRALIA

ANTARCTICA

The Atmosphere The envelope of gases surrounding Earth is called the **atmosphere.** The air you breathe is part of the atmosphere. Nitrogen and oxygen make up most of the atmosphere. Organisms need these and other gases to live. The atmosphere also helps protect living things by blocking harmful rays given off by the Sun. These rays, called ultraviolet rays, cause sunburn, skin cancer, and eye damage.

 IDENTIFY: What are the two main gases in Earth's atmosphere?

✓ CHECKING CONCEPTS

1. The ground you walk on is part of the _____.
2. The air you breathe is part of the _____.
3. The _____ includes rivers, lakes, and oceans.
4. Earth is a round, three-dimensional object known as a _____.
5. Salt water makes up about _____ percent of the hydrosphere.
6. There are _____ continents on Earth.
7. There are _____ major oceans on Earth.

💡 THINKING CRITICALLY

8. **INTERPRET:** Use Figure 1-5 to answer the following questions:

   a. Which is the smallest continent?

   b. Which is the largest continent?

9. **ANALYZE:** Draw a pie graph that shows the percentages of salt water and fresh water on Earth.

BUILDING READING SKILLS

Using Prefixes Prefixes are word parts that appear at the beginning of words. Prefixes have consistent meanings. Knowing the definition of a prefix can help you figure out the meaning of a particular word. Two prefixes that are used often in this lesson are *litho-* and *hydro-*. Find out the meanings of these prefixes. (Hint: *Litho* is defined in this lesson.) Then, figure out and write down the definitions of the following words that use these prefixes: *hydroelectric, hydrologist, lithology,* and *lithographer.* Circle the part of the definition that relates to each prefix. Put each word in a sentence.

Integrating Life Science

TOPIC: biosphere

LIFE ON EARTH

The part of Earth that supports all living things is called the biosphere. Parts of the lithosphere, the hydrosphere, and the atmosphere make up the biosphere.

The biosphere is a very narrow zone. You may think living things are almost everywhere. Some kinds of clams live in deep-sea vents on the ocean floor. Some spiders live high in the atmosphere. Bacteria are found deep in the crust. The biosphere extends 8 to 10 km into the atmosphere. Yet compared to the entire volume of Earth, the part where life exists is very small.

Thinking Critically Why do you think life is found only in the biosphere?

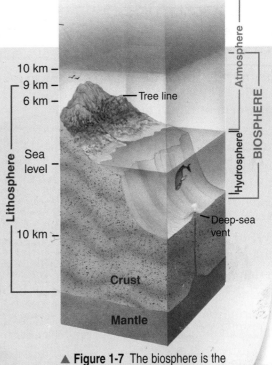

▲ **Figure 1-7** The biosphere is the part of Earth where life exists.

What is the structure of Earth?

INVESTIGATE

Modeling Earth's Layers
HANDS-ON ACTIVITY

1. Cut a hard-boiled egg in half with the shell still on it.
⚠ **CAUTION:** Be very careful when working with sharp objects.

2. On three small pieces of paper or self-stick labels, write "Yolk," "White," and "Shell." Tape the papers to three thin straws or coffee stirrers or fold the self-stick labels around them. Use the straws or stirrers to label each part of the egg.

THINK ABOUT IT: Like the egg, Earth has a core, material around the core, and a thin but hard outer skin. Which parts of the model are like Earth's outer skin, middle, and core?

STEP 2

Objective

Describe Earth's major parts: the crust, the mantle, and the core.

Key Terms

crust: solid, thin outer layer of Earth

mantle (MAN-tuhl)**:** thick layer of rock below the crust

core: innermost region of Earth

A Slightly Flat Sphere

A perfect sphere has no real top. Every point on the surface of a sphere is the same distance from the center. Earth is a sphere, but not a perfect one. It is slightly squashed, or flat, at its poles. Also, Earth bulges out a little around its middle. Diameter is the distance across a sphere through its center. Earth is about 12,756 km in diameter at the equator. The diameter of Earth from pole to pole is about 12,664 km.

▲ **Figure 1-8** The outline of Earth does not fit perfectly into the outline of a sphere.

▶ **EXPLAIN:** How is Earth not a perfect sphere?

Earth's Crust

What is below Earth's surface? Like the hard-boiled egg above, Earth has three basic layers: the crust, the mantle, and the core. The **crust** is the thin, outer layer of Earth. It forms the upper lithosphere. Beneath the oceans, the crust is from 5 to 10 km thick. However, beneath the continents, the crust is from 32 to 70 km thick. The thickest crust is beneath mountains.

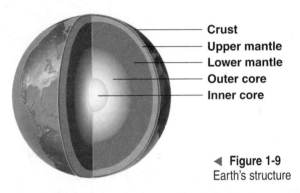

Crust
Upper mantle
Lower mantle
Outer core
Inner core

◀ **Figure 1-9** Earth's structure

2 **CONTRAST:** How is ocean crust different from continental crust?

Earth's Mantle

The layer of Earth beneath the crust is called the **mantle.** Earth's mantle ranges from about 1,800 to 2,900 km thick. More than two-thirds of the mass of Earth is in the mantle.

The lithosphere includes all of the crust and the upper part of the mantle. Below this, the rock flows like a very thick liquid. Most of the mantle is made up of rock that flows very slowly.

3 **OBSERVE:** Where is the mantle located?

Earth's Core The innermost region of Earth is the **core.** Scientists think that the core is made mostly of iron. The core has two parts. The outer core is liquid. It is about 2,250 km thick. The inner core is solid, with a radius of about 1,300 km.

THE LAYERS OF EARTH	
Layer	Thickness
Crust	5–70 km
Mantle	2,900 km
Outer Core	2,250 km
Inner Core	1,300 km

▲ Figure 1-10

 CALCULATE: Which is thicker, the mantle or the two core layers combined?

 CHECKING CONCEPTS

1. The crust is thickest beneath _____.
2. The core is made mostly of _____.

3. You can stand on Earth's layer called the _____.

4. The diameter of Earth at the equator is about _____ km.

THINKING CRITICALLY

5. **SEQUENCE:** Arrange Earth's layers in order, from thickest to thinnest.

6. **ANALYZE:** A drilling rig can go down only 6 km. Where would you set it up to drill into the mantle? Why?

7. **INFER:** Which layer of Earth includes the continents?

BUILDING MATH SKILLS

Calculating The radius, or *r*, of Earth is the point measured from its center to its surface. Use the formula below to find the approximate circumference, or *C*, of Earth. Pi, or π, is equal to 3.14. $C = 2 \pi r$.

How Do They Know That?

EARTH IS A SPHERE

For thousands of years, people believed Earth was flat. This seemed logical. If you stand in a field or sail on the ocean, you can see for many kilometers. Everything appears flat. About 2,500 years ago, around 500 B.C., the Greek philosopher Pythagoras suggested that Earth was a sphere. His idea was probably based on observing the night sky. The heights of stars in the sky varied, depending on where you stood on Earth's surface. The Moon appeared to be round. Possibly, Earth had the same shape.

Many years later, another Greek philosopher, Aristotle, supported Pythagoras' theory. While observing lunar eclipses, Aristotle noted that a curved shadow fell on the Moon. He believed this to be Earth's shadow. Aristotle concluded that Earth was round.

Today, pictures from space show us that Earth is indeed a sphere.

Thinking Critically How did Pythagoras' observation of the heights of stars support his theory?

▲ Figure 1-11 Pythagoras (c. 580 B.C. to c. 500 B.C.), Greek philosopher and mathematician

What are maps?

Objectives

Explain why a globe is the most useful type of Earth map. Describe what happens when the round Earth is shown on a flat map.

Key Terms

globe: three-dimensional model of Earth's surface

map: flat model of Earth's surface

distortion (dih-STAWR-shuhn): error in shape, size, or distance

Globes A **globe** is a three-dimensional model of Earth's surface. A model is something that represents a real object such as a ship or an airplane. A globe correctly shows the shapes and sizes of features on Earth. For this reason, a globe is the best model of Earth. Most globes, however, are too small to show much detail. Larger globes are too big to handle. Imagine trying to carry a globe to school every day!

◀ **Figure 1-12** Globes are good models of Earth's surface. However, they can be hard to carry around.

▶ DEFINE: What is a globe?

Maps A **map** is a flat model, or drawing, of Earth's surface. It is two-dimensional. There are many kinds of maps.

Some maps show the whole Earth. Other maps show only part of Earth. Maps that show a small part of Earth can show more details than maps that show more of Earth.

Maps can show many different things. They can show the locations of and distances between places on Earth. Some maps show city streets. Other maps show buildings in a town. Some maps even show the weather or types of soil in an area.

▲ **Figure 1-13** Navigation systems in cars display maps that help you find your way in a strange city.

▶ IDENTIFY: What features are shown on maps?

Distortion When a round surface such as Earth is shown on a flat map, errors occur. If the shapes on the map are correct, the distances may be wrong. If the distances are correct, the shapes may be wrong. These errors in shape, size, or distance are called **distortions.** Nearly all maps have some distortions. Maps of smaller areas have fewer distortions.

▲ **Figure 1-14** Maps can vary in how much detail they show.

▶ COMPARE: Which would have more distortions, a map of the United States or a map of Florida? Explain.

✔ CHECKING CONCEPTS

1. A map is a _____ model of Earth.
2. The best model of Earth is a _____.
3. Errors on a map are called _____.

💡 THINKING CRITICALLY

4. EXPLAIN: Why is a globe the best model of Earth?
5. HYPOTHESIZE: When would a flat map be more useful than a globe?
6. APPLY: Globes and maps can be used to find the distances between different places. Maria wanted to know how far it was from her house to her friend's house in the next town. She tried to use a globe to find out. Why might Maria have a problem using a globe to find the distance between the two towns?

BUILDING SCIENCE SKILLS

Modeling and Comparing Using an 8 ½ × 11 inch sheet of paper, make a map of your classroom.

1. Measure 2 cm from each edge of the paper to draw the walls of the room.
2. Fold the paper into quarters and then open it. Use these folds as guides.
3. Draw as many objects as you can in each part. Draw where you and your teacher sit.
4. Have a classmate locate places in the room on your map. Does your map have distortion? Indicate where in your map any distortion might be and why.

Science and Technology

EARTH-OBSERVATION SATELLITES

Landsat is the oldest U.S. land-surface observation satellite system. The satellites orbit from pole to pole. They use remote sensing to collect information about Earth's surface. Remote sensing is the ability to gather information about an object or event without actually being in physical contact with it. A *Landsat* satellite can provide images with great detail. Images from *Landsat* have been used to map wildfire hazards in Yosemite National Park; track lava flows in Hawaii; and observe population growth in large U.S. cities.

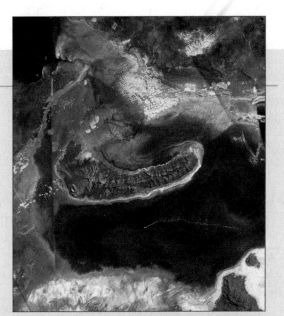

▲ **Figure 1-15** This satellite image shows Salt Lake City in Utah.

The National Aeronautics and Space Administration, or NASA, launched the first *Landsat* satellite more than 30 years ago. Before it was retired, it had recorded over 300,000 images. Since then, at least seven more *Landsats* have been launched. Most of the launches were successful.

Other observation satellite systems are *SarSat* and *NavStar*. *NavStar* is made up of 24 satellites that orbit Earth over different areas. The system is used today to keep track of airplane traffic. It is also used to help during search and rescue missions. *SarSat* is an international search and rescue satellite system.

Thinking Critically Why do you think it is important to track wildfire hazards in a national park?

1-5 What is a map projection?

INVESTIGATE

Making a Map Projection
HANDS-ON ACTIVITY

1. Look at a globe. With a felt-tip pen or permanent marker, roughly outline the continents on the surface of a grapefruit.

2. Carefully cut the grapefruit into quarters. Gently peel the skin off the grapefruit. Try not to tear the four pieces of peel into smaller pieces.

3. Lay the four pieces of peel flat on a table. Match up your pieces to form a flat map.

THINK ABOUT IT: What happens to the continents when you try to flatten the pieces? How can you adjust them to make them match better?

STEP 1

Objectives
Explain what a map projection is. Name three kinds of map projections.

Key Term
map projection (proh-JEHK-shuhn)**:** drawing of Earth's surface, or part of it, on a flat surface

From Round to Flat A **map projection** is a flat map that represents all or part of Earth's curved surface. Imagine a clear plastic globe with a light inside. If paper is wrapped around the lighted globe, the outlines of the continents will be projected onto the paper. A mapmaker can trace these outlines to make a flat map. The result is called a map projection.

 DEFINE: What is a map projection?

Types of Map Projections There are several types of map projections. Although no type is completely accurate, each kind is useful.

Gerardus Mercator (1512–1594) was a Flemish cartographer, or mapmaker. He drew a huge world map in 1569 that used the system of projection now named for him. Mercator was one of the most respected geographers of his time.

Mercator projections are made by wrapping a sheet of paper into a tube around a globe. An example is shown in Figure 1-16. In a Mercator projection, the distances between land areas and the sizes of land areas near the poles are distorted.

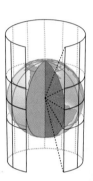

▲ **Figure 1-16** A Mercator projection

A polar projection, shown in Figure 1-17, is made by holding a flat sheet of paper on one pole of a globe. It shows little distortion near that pole. Farther from that pole, however, both direction and distance are distorted.

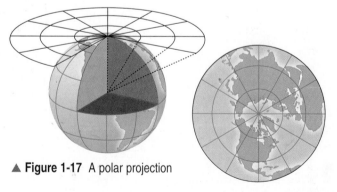

▲ **Figure 1-17** A polar projection

A conic (KAHN-ik) projection is shown in Figure 1-18. It is made by shaping a sheet of paper into a cone and placing it over a globe. When several conic projections are put together, the relative shapes and sizes of land areas on the map are almost the same as those on a globe.

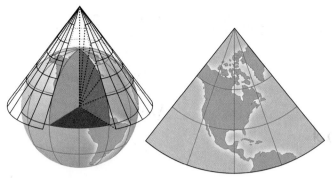

▲ **Figure 1-18** A conic projection

 INFER: Which kind of map projection would you use to explore Antarctica?

☑ CHECKING CONCEPTS

1. What is a flat map of a curved surface called?
2. How is a Mercator projection made?
3. How is a conic projection made?
4. How do mapmakers show Earth's surface on a flat map?
5. How is a polar projection made?

💡 THINKING CRITICALLY

6. **INFER:** Why do you think a conic projection and a polar projection are called by these names?

Web InfoSearch

Mercator Projections Mercator projections are very helpful to navigators at sea. They are widely used to create navigation charts. On Mercator projections, lines of latitude and longitude are straight, parallel lines. This allows a navigator to plot a straight course.

SEARCH: Use the Internet to find out more. How does a sailor use one to plot a course? What problems would occur if the sailor were heading for the poles? Start your search at www.conceptsandchallenges.com. Some key search words are **sailing projections** and **Mercator projections.**

 How Do They Know That?

LOCATING FEATURES ON EARTH'S SURFACE

When do you think the first maps were made? The earliest known maps are more than 4,000 years old. These early maps were carved on clay tablets. Maps during this time showed rivers, mountains, and human settlements. They may have been used to record property lines and help build roads, canals, and towns.

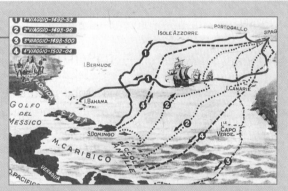

▲ **Figure 1-19** This early map shows the various routes Columbus took to reach and return from the New World.

The first people to show Earth as a sphere on maps were the Greeks. About A.D. 100, Ptolemy (TAHL-uh-mee), an Egyptian astronomer, mathematician, and geographer, wrote a book based on Greek ideas called *Geography*. In this book, he described how to make maps and globes. Columbus may have used Ptolemy's maps when he set out on his voyage to the New World.

During the fifteenth and sixteenth centuries, the explorations of Columbus, Da Gama, and Magellan led to more accurate maps of Earth. The most famous mapmaker during this time was Mercator. Today, aerial photographs, satellites, and computers are all used to make detailed, accurate maps of Earth's surface.

Thinking Critically How has technology helped us make more accurate maps of Earth's surface?

1-6 What are latitude and longitude?

Objective

Explain how hemispheres, latitude, longitude, meridians, and parallels are all related.

Key Terms

parallel (PAR-uh-lehl): horizontal line on a map or globe that circles Earth from east to west at intervals starting at the equator

latitude (LAT-uh-tood): distance in degrees north or south of the equator

meridian (muh-RIHD-ee-uhn): line on a map or globe running from the North Pole to the South Pole along Earth's surface

longitude (LAHN-juh-tood): measurement in degrees east or west of the prime meridian

Parallels and Meridians If you look at a globe or a map of the world, you will notice a series of lines drawn east and west and another series drawn north and south. These reference lines help people describe locations anywhere on Earth's surface. One handy reference is the equator. The equator is an imaginary line that runs around the middle of Earth's surface. It divides Earth into two half-spheres—the Northern Hemisphere and the Southern Hemisphere. As shown in Figure 1-20, angles drawn from Earth's center to its surface are used to construct other east-west lines on Earth's surface. **Parallels** are lines on maps and globes that circle Earth east to west parallel to the equator.

Another set of lines on maps and globes, called meridians, run north and south across Earth's surface. A **meridian** is a half-circle that extends from the North Pole to the South Pole. Figure 1-21 shows how meridians are constructed.

▶ 1 COMPARE/CONTRAST: How are parallels and meridians similar? How are they different?

Latitude Parallels and meridians are used to describe locations on Earth's surface. Parallels describe latitude. **Latitude** is the distance in degrees north and south of the equator. The latitude of the equator is 0°.

The North Pole is at 90° north latitude. The South Pole is at 90° south latitude. Figure 1-20 shows how the locations of latitude lines are determined.

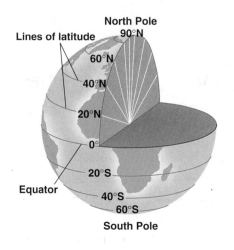

◀ **Figure 1-20**
Lines of latitude run horizontally around the globe.

▶ 2 MEASURE: What is the latitude of the equator?

Longitude Meridians are used to describe longitude. **Longitude** is the distance in degrees east and west of the 0° meridian. Since there is no equator dividing Earth into north-south halves, scientists had to invent one. This 0° meridian, which runs through Greenwich, England, is called the prime meridian. On the other side of Earth from the prime meridian is the 180° meridian. Called the International Date Line, this is the place where the calendar day changes. Figure 1-21 shows how longitude lines are drawn.

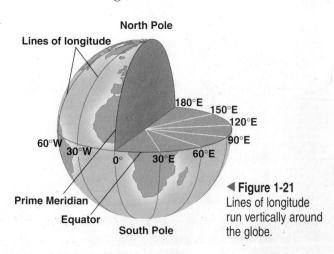

◀ **Figure 1-21**
Lines of longitude run vertically around the globe.

▶ 3 NAME: What is the name of the meridian that passes through Greenwich, England?

Locating Places Every place on Earth has its own latitude and longitude. For example, Washington, D.C., is very close to the point where the parallel for 39° north meets the meridian for 70° west. So, Washington's location can be described as 39° north latitude and 70° west longitude. This number can be abbreviated as 39°N, 70°W.

▶ **4** COMPARE: What describes the location of a place?

✓ CHECKING CONCEPTS

1. The parallel around the middle of Earth is the _____.

2. Each half of Earth's surface is called a _____.

3. Points on a sphere or angles in a circle are measured in units called _____.

4. Lines running horizontally on a map or globe are called _____.

5. Lines running from pole to pole on a map or globe are called _____.

THINKING CRITICALLY

6. EXPLAIN: How can you locate a particular city on a map of Earth's surface?

7. NAME: In what place on Earth's surface is there a latitude of 0° and a longitude of 0°?

8. INFER: What do you think the hemispheres formed by the prime meridian and the International Date Line are called?

9. INFER: What is the North Pole's latitude and longitude?

BUILDING SCIENCE SKILLS

Locating Use a globe or a map to identify the cities with the following latitudes and longitudes.

IDENTIFYING CITIES		
City	Latitude	Longitude
A	38° N	77° W
B	30° N	90° W
C	35° N	140°E

▲ **Figure 1-22**

Hands-On Activity

FINDING PLACES ON A MAP

1. Find the following cities on the map:
   New Orleans, LA
   Pittsburgh, PA
   San Antonio, TX
   Jacksonville, FL
   Springfield, IL
   Denver, CO

2. Write the latitude and longitude of each city. Estimate as closely as possible.

▲ **Figure 1-23** Latitudes and longitudes in the United States

Practicing Your Skills

3. EXPLAIN: Why do you need to know both latitude and longitude to locate places on a map?

4. IDENTIFY: What is the approximate latitude and longitude of the city where you live?

Objectives

Use the scale on a map. Interpret map symbols.

Key Terms

scale: feature that relates distances on a map to actual distances on Earth's surface

symbol: drawing on a map that represents a real object

legend (LEHJ-uhnd): list of map symbols and their meanings

Showing Direction Most maps show directions. If you look at the map on this page, you will see an arrow marked N. This arrow shows the direction north. On most maps, north (N) is at the top of the map. From this you can infer that south (S) is at the bottom, east (E) is to your right, and west (W) is to your left.

Another way of showing direction on a map is using a compass rose. Most places on a map are not exactly north, south, east, or west. In Figure 1-24, you can see that Snake River flows both south and north and east and west. The direction between south and west is called southwest (SW). The direction between north and east is called northeast (NE).

A compass rose is a circle divided into eighths. It shows the four directions and directions in between the four.

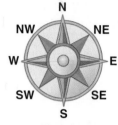

▲ **Figure 1-25** Compass rose

1️⃣ **OBSERVE:** On a map, what shows the direction?

Scale A map's **scale** shows how the distance on the map compares with real distance on Earth's surface. Look at the scale in Figure 1-24. It shows that 1 cm on the map equals 5 km on Earth's surface. Measure the distance on the map from Point A to Point B. The distance is 4.4 cm. To find the actual distance between Point A and Point B, multiply 4.4 × 5, because each centimeter on the map represents 5 km on Earth. On Earth's surface, the actual distance from Point A to Point B is 22 km.

2️⃣ **CALCULATE:** The main street in a town is 10 km long. How many centimeters would the street be on a map that uses the scale 1 cm = 5 km?

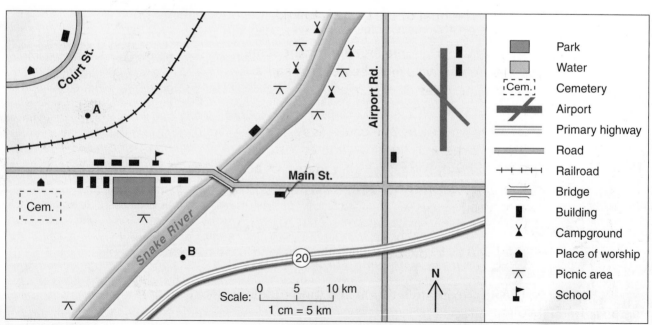

⬛	Park
⬜	Water
⌜Cem.⌝	Cemetery
✖	Airport
══	Primary highway
──	Road
+++++	Railroad
⎓	Bridge
∎	Building
Y	Campground
▲	Place of worship
⊼	Picnic area
⌐	School

▲ **Figure 1-24** Town map

Map Symbols Simple drawings on a map called **symbols** are used to show the location of real objects. Many different symbols are used on maps. These symbols are listed in a table called a **legend.** Different maps have different legends. The legend of each map explains the symbols used on that map. See the legend in Figure 1-24 for some common map symbols.

 ANALYZE: Why are symbols used on a map?

Color Color often has meaning on maps. Black is usually used for anything made by people. Symbols for buildings, railroads, and bridges are colored black. Blue is used to show bodies of water. Forests and parks are green.

4 **IDENTIFY:** What color would be used to show your school on a map?

 CHECKING CONCEPTS

1. The direction northwest would be shown on a map by the letters _____.
2. The _____ on a map shows distance.
3. Simple drawings on a map used to show real objects are called _____.

4. The symbols used on a map are listed in a _____.
5. A river would most likely be colored _____ on a map.

 THINKING CRITICALLY

6. **CLASSIFY:** What types of information do the scale and the legend on a map provide?
7. **MODEL:** Draw a simple map of the area around your school. Include a scale and a legend of all the symbols you think belong there.

INTERPRETING VISUALS

Use Figure 1-24 to answer the following questions.

8. **OBSERVE:** How many buildings are shown on the map?
9. **OBSERVE:** What kinds of buildings and roads are shown?
10. **ANALYZE:** What direction is to your left on the map?
11. **ANALYZE:** In what two directions does Main Street run?

Real-Life Science
ORIENTEERING

Orienteering is a fun sport. The goal of the game is to find specific areas marked on a given course. As you move through the course, you race against other people looking for the same marked points as you are. To win, you must be able to read a map quickly and use a compass. Classes in map and compass reading are offered at some orienteering meets.

Before an orienteering meet begins, the course is set up. Markers are left at different checkpoints along the course. Each orienteering participant is given a map that identifies all of the checkpoints. The first person to cross the finish line with each checkpoint marker wins.

You can participate in orienteering meets no matter where you live. Courses have been set up in cities as well as in wooded areas. You do not need any special equipment except a map and compass.

Thinking Critically What checkpoints might there be along a city orienteering course?

▲ **Figure 1-26** Orienteering courses can be found in many places. There are even orienteering courses set up for disabled athletes.

THE Big IDEA

How did maps help the United States grow?

Look at a modern map of the United States. You will see a vast stretch of land extending from the Atlantic Ocean to the Pacific Ocean and from Canada to the Gulf of Mexico. A map of what the United States looked like in 1800 would look very different. The country then was only about one-third of its current size. It consisted of lands that extended westward from the Atlantic Ocean to the Mississippi River.

President Thomas Jefferson dreamed of an America that would stretch from sea to sea. In 1803, he bought from France all of the lands between the Mississippi River and the Rocky Mountains. This so-called Louisiana Purchase doubled the size of the country. The United States paid only $15 million for this land.

No maps of the area existed. Jefferson decided to send explorers to map the region and report on local wildlife and climate. He asked his personal secretary, Meriwether Lewis, to lead the expedition. Lewis asked his friend, William Clark, to join him.

In 1804, the two men left St. Louis with 28 others. The group, known as the Corps of Discovery, arrived back home 2½ years later. The maps, charts, and journals they brought back opened the door to westward expansion.

Look at the illustrations that appear on these two pages. Then, follow the directions in the Science Log to learn more about "the big idea." ✦

Spring 1805

Lewis climbs to the top of a hill and views the Rocky Mountains for the first time.

Winter 1806

The expedition spends the harsh winter months at Fort Clatsop in present-day Oregon. Lewis and Clark make sketches of wildlife and of the Native Americans living in this previously unexplored area. This is a sample from their journal.

Ft. Clatsop

N

Pacific Ocean

WRITING ACTIVITY

Science Log

You are traveling with the Corps of Discovery. On your journey, you observe many strange new animals and eat new foods. You view the Rocky Mountains for the first time. Write down your observations. Draw a simple map with a legend of the place you are describing. Start your search at www.conceptsandchallenges.com.

Winter 1805

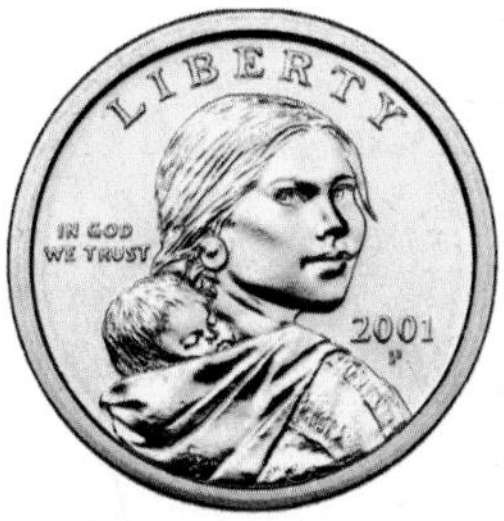
LIBERTY
IN GOD WE TRUST
2001
P

The Corps of Discovery sets up winter quarters near present-day Bismarck, North Dakota. During this time, Toussaint Charbonneau joins the group as an interpreter. His wife, a Shoshone named Sacagawea (sac-a-juh-WEE-ah), also joins the expedition as a guide. She is honored on the coin shown.

Fall 1804

The explorers leave the trail and meet the Arikara. Clark records information about this Plains group in his journal. He notes that the Arikara are farmers who live year round in earthen lodges.

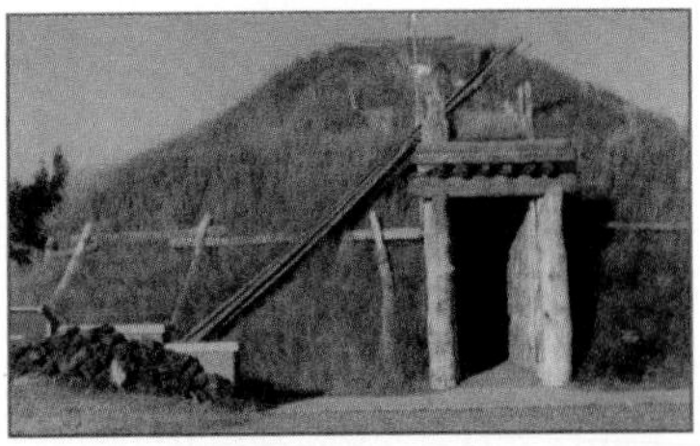

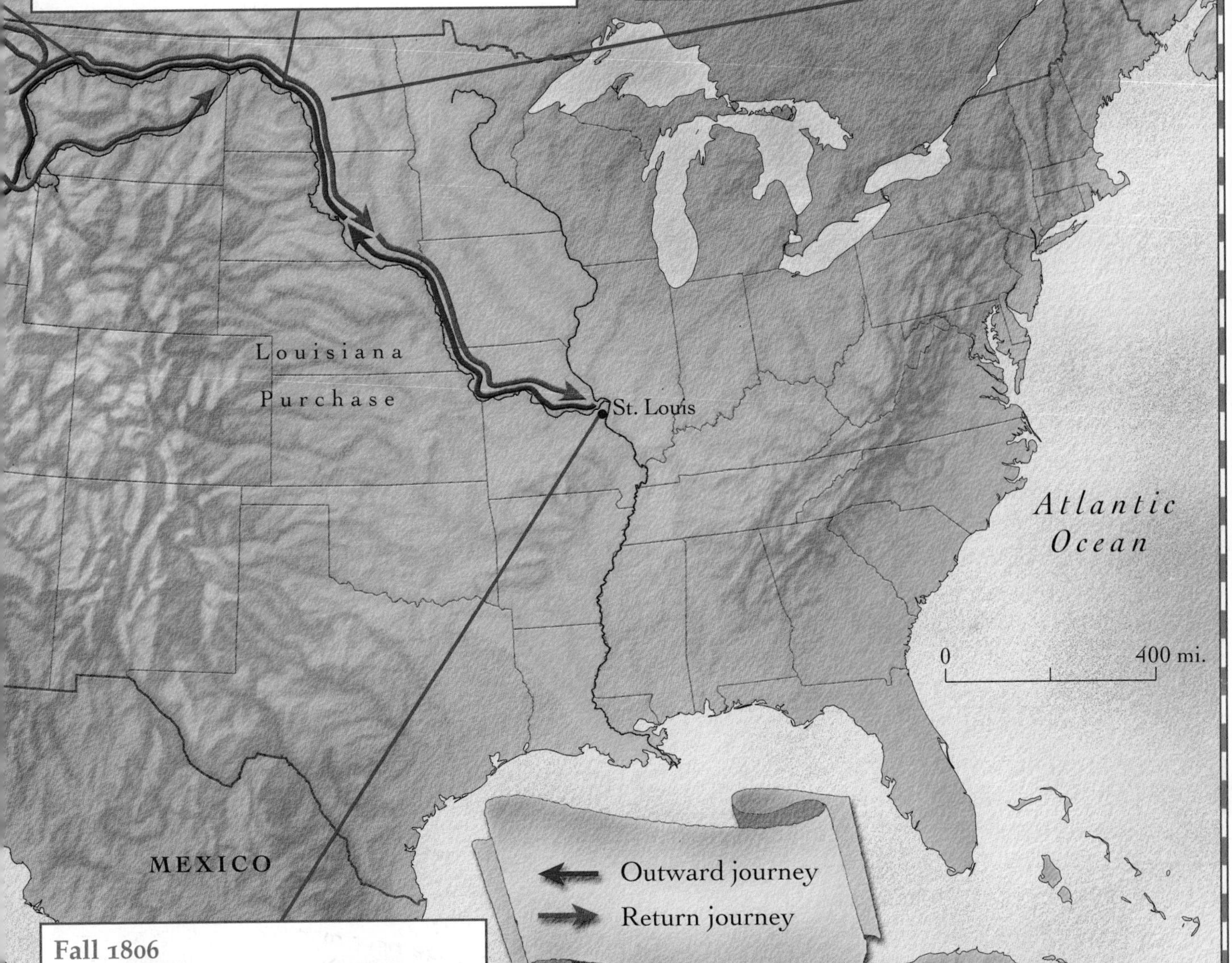
Louisiana Purchase
St. Louis
Atlantic Ocean
MEXICO
0
400 mi.
Outward journey
Return journey

Fall 1806

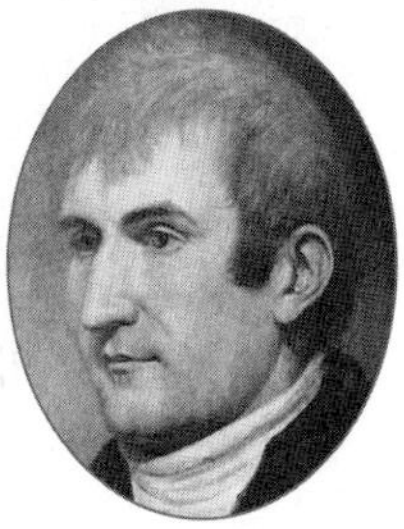

M. Lewis

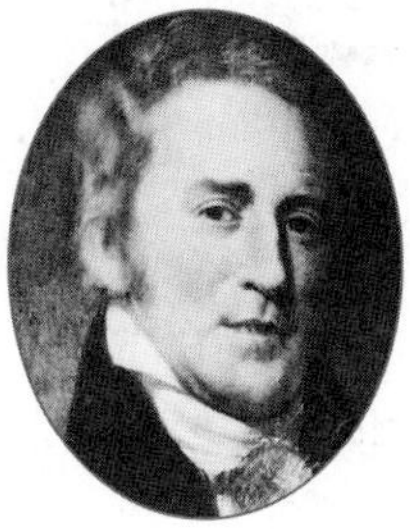

W. Clark

The explorers arrive back in St. Louis on September 23. The whole town turns out to give them a heroes' welcome.

▲ **Figure 1-27** This map of the early United States shows the travel route of Lewis and Clark. The maps Lewis and Clark created led to the expansion of the western United States.

1-8 What is a topographic map?

Objective
Describe what is shown on a topographic map.

Key Terms
elevation (el-uh-VAY-shuhn): height of a point on Earth above or below sea level

topography (tuh-PAHG-ruh-fee): general form and shape of the land on Earth's surface

contour (KAHN-toor) **line:** line drawn on a map that connects all points having the same elevation

Elevation The level of the water in the oceans is about the same height everywhere on Earth. The average height for water in the oceans is called sea level. The height of a place on land is measured from sea level. For example, the height of Mount McKinley, Alaska, is more than 6 km above sea level. The height of land above or below sea level is called **elevation.**

▶ **1** DEFINE: What is elevation?

Topography The general form and shape of the land on Earth's surface is called **topography.** Examples of topography on Earth's surface are mountains, valleys, plains, and plateaus. Mountains have high elevations and steep slopes. Valleys are low areas bordered by high ground. Plains are broad, flat areas that are usually only a little above sea level. Plateaus are broad, flat areas of land that have an elevation of at least 300 m above sea level.

▶ **2** IDENTIFY: What are three types of topography on Earth's surface?

Contour Lines The elevations of surface features can be shown on a map using contour lines. A **contour line** is a line that passes through all points on a map that have the same elevation. When you look at the contour lines on a map, you can identify the shape, or contour, of the land. Every point on a contour line has the same elevation.

▶ **3** DESCRIBE: What do contour lines on a map show?

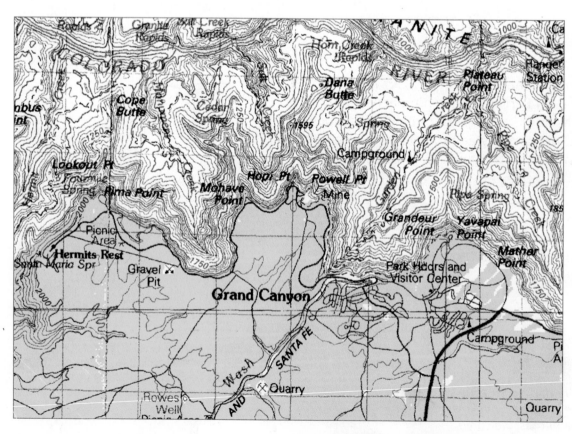

◀ **Figure 1-28**
A topographic map, like the one to the left, shows surface features such as differences in elevation.

Topographic Maps A map with contour lines shows the surface features, or topography, of the land. That is why these maps are called topographic maps. The contour lines found on a topographic map connect places on the map having the same elevation. Figure 1-28 is a topographic map of the Grand Canyon area in Arizona.

 EXPLAIN: What is a topographic map?

 CHECKING CONCEPTS

1. What is sea level?
2. What is topography?
3. What is a contour line?
4. What is the height of a point above or below sea level called?

 THINKING CRITICALLY

5. **CONTRAST:** What is the difference between sea level and elevation?
6. **EXPLAIN:** A contour line is marked 50 m. What does this mean?

7. **INFER:** Why are plateaus sometimes called "plains in the air?"
8. **RELATE:** Why is a map with contour lines called a topographic map?

Web InfoSearch

Contour Plowing Farmers planting on hilly ground are careful to plow their land in a special way. They plow along strips of land that are at the same elevation. In this way, all the furrows follow the slope of the hill. Water collects in the furrows and soaks into the soil. The furrows prevent the water from running down the hill and carrying away valuable topsoil. This kind of plowing is called contour plowing.

SEARCH: Use the Internet to find out more about contour plowing. In what countries is it used? Why? Start your search at **www.conceptsandchallenges.com**. Some key search words are **agriculture, farming, topsoil,** and **contour tilling.**

People in Science

SURVEYOR

A surveyor measures land to find the exact location of certain physical features on Earth's surface. Engineers employ surveyors to measure the heights of objects, the slope of the land, and the distances between physical features. With this information, engineers design roads, bridges, and homes.

Ken Stigner began his surveying career in the military. He prepared maps for the construction of roads and bridges. He started as a member of a crew taking measurements ("chain man"). Then, he became an instrument operator. Later, he was made party chief. This meant he had his own crew.

▲ **Figure 1-29** Surveyors use many different tools, such as this transit, when working on building projects.

Surveyors come from all education levels. Some have little education and just want to work outdoors. Although on-the-job training is possible, it helps to have a background in mathematics. It requires many years of experience to obtain a surveying license. Some states now require a four-year degree in surveying to qualify.

Thinking Critically Why do you think the military may need to build roads and bridges?

How do you read a topographic map?

Contour Intervals A topographic map shows the elevation of features on Earth's surface. Look at the topographic map shown in Figure 1-30. Every point on a contour line is at the same elevation.

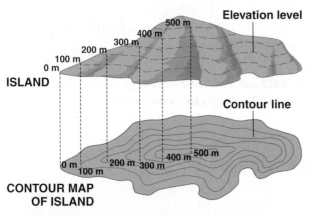

▲ **Figure 1-30** This drawing shows how an island's different elevations would look on a topographic map.

The places where contour lines are close together, the land has a steep slope. The places where the lines are far apart, the land has a gentle slope.

The difference in elevation between one contour line and the next is called a **contour interval.** If two contour lines near each other are marked 500 and 600 m, the contour interval between them is 100 m. Mapmakers use different contour intervals for different maps. A large contour interval is used for mountainous areas. A small contour interval is used for flat areas.

1 OBSERVE: What is the contour interval for the map in Figure 1-30?

Relief Map A map that uses color, shading, or contour lines to indicate the different heights of features is called a relief map. On a relief map, like the one in Figure 1-31, one color might be used to show high mountains. Another color might be used to show areas near sea level. Still other colors might be used to show elevations in between or for areas below sea level.

2 EXPLAIN: How is color sometimes used to show elevation on a relief map?

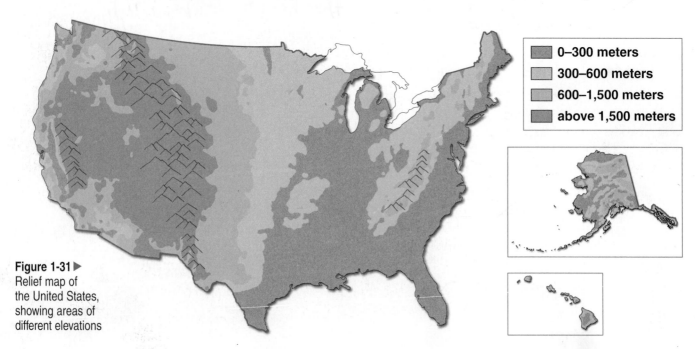

0–300 meters
300–600 meters
600–1,500 meters
above 1,500 meters

Figure 1-31 ▶
Relief map of the United States, showing areas of different elevations

☑ CHECKING CONCEPTS

1. Where contour lines are close together, the land has a _____ slope.

2. The difference in elevation between two neighboring contour lines is called the _____.

3. A map of a flat area would usually have a _____ contour interval.

4. Instead of contour lines, some maps use _____ to show elevation.

THINKING CRITICALLY

Use Figures 1-30 and 1-31 to answer the following questions.

5. **OBSERVE:** What is the highest elevation shown in Figure 1-30?

6. **ANALYZE:** Is the land shown in Figure 1-30 flat or hilly? How do you know?

7. **OBSERVE:** What color is used in Figure 1-31 to show elevations from 0 to 300 m?

8. **ANALYZE:** What is the elevation of the land shown in dark green in Figure 1-31?

INTERPRETING VISUALS

Reading a Topographic Map The symbol X on a topographic map is called a benchmark. A benchmark is a mark on a map that shows a landmark with a known height. The landmark is used as a reference point in relation to the height of other things on the map. A depression is shown on a topographic map by using short, straight lines pointing toward the center of the depression. Look at Figure 1-32. Which point on the map is the benchmark? What is the elevation at the benchmark? Which point shows a depression?

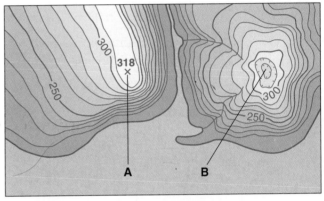

▲ **Figure 1-32** Elevation is shown in meters.

Hands-On Activity

INTERPRETING A TOPOGRAPHIC MAP

You will need a pencil, a sheet of paper, and a metric ruler. Examine the map in Figure 1-33. Then, answer the following questions.

Practicing Your Skills

1. **IDENTIFY:** What contour interval is used on the map in Figure 1-33?

2. **CALCULATE:** What are the elevations of Points *A*, *B*, and *C*?

3. **CALCULATE:** How many meters is the highest point on the map?

4. **MEASURE:** How long in meters is the river?

5. **INFER:** The hill shown on the map has three sides that are steep and one side that is gentle. How can you tell which are the steep sides and which is the gentle side? What is the compass direction of the gentle side of the hill?

6. **ANALYZE:** Which letter is in a depression? How do you know?

▲ **Figure 1-33** The contour lines on this map show several land features.

LAB ACTIVITY
Making a Topographic Map

Materials

Lab apron
Gloves (optional)
Modeling clay
Thread
   (about 30 cm long)
Plain paper
Pencil
Metric ruler

▲ **STEP 2** Shape your clay to form a mountain.

▲ **STEP 3** Push a pencil down through the top of your mountain.

BACKGROUND

Earth's surface is covered with mountains, valleys, plateaus, and broad plains. Topographic maps show these features. They contain contour lines. These lines show the look and shape of the land.

PURPOSE

In this activity, you will shape a clay model of a mountain. You will then construct a topographic map of your model.

PROCEDURE

1. Put on your lab apron.

2. Place a sheet of plain paper on your desk. Put a lump of clay in the middle of the paper. Shape the clay to form a mountain and a valley. Make the mountain 8 cm high.

3. Push a pencil through the top of your mountain all the way down to the paper to make a mark. Pull the pencil out. Make a second hole about 2 cm from the first hole. Make a mark on the paper. Pull out the pencil.

4. Stand a ruler beside your mountain. Mark your clay at a height of 7 cm.

5. Hold both ends of the thread tightly so it is parallel to the table. Slice the top of the mountain off at the 7-cm mark you just made. Remove it and set it aside.

6. Now, measure and mark a 6-cm height on the mountain. Using the thread again, slice the mountain off at the 6-cm mark. Set this piece aside.

7. Repeat Steps 4 and 5 for heights of 5, 4, 3, 2, and 1 cm.

8. Use your pencil to trace a line around the bottom slice of the mountain. This is a contour line.

9. Remove the bottom slice from the paper. Place the slice that was on top of the bottom slice on the paper. Line up both holes in the slice with the pencil marks on the paper. Trace around this slice and remove it.

10. Trace around each of the remaining four slices using the same paper. Be sure to line up both holes before you trace.

11. Rebuild your clay mountain by stacking all the pieces back together in order from largest to smallest. Compare your mountain to the topographic map you just drew.

▲ **STEP 7** Slice off marked sections of the mountain.

▲ **STEP 10** Trace around your slices.

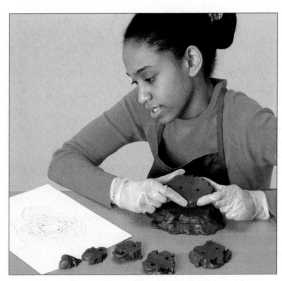

▲ **STEP 11** Rebuild your clay mountain.

CONCLUSIONS

1. **ANALYZE:** What do the contour lines on the topographic map show?
2. **OBSERVE:** What do widely spread contour lines tell you about the shape of the land?
3. **OBSERVE:** What do closely spaced contour lines tell you about the shape of the land?
4. **INFER:** How do you think geologists use topographic maps?

Chapter Summary

Lesson 1-1

- **Earth science** is the study of Earth and its history. The four branches of Earth science are geology, oceanography, meteorology, and astronomy.

Lesson 1-2

- A **sphere** is a round, three-dimensional object. The **lithosphere** is the solid part of Earth. The **hydrosphere** is made of liquid water or ice. The **atmosphere** is an envelope of gases surrounding Earth.

Lesson 1-3

- Earth has three layers. The **crust** is the outer layer. The **mantle** is below the crust. Its upper part is solid rock. The rock below this flows like a thick liquid. The **core** in the center has an outer liquid layer and an inner solid layer.

Lessons 1-4 and 1-5

- A **globe** is a spherical model of Earth. A **map** is a flat model of Earth. All maps have **distortions.**
- A **map projection** shows Earth's surface, or part of it, on a sheet of paper. Three examples of map projections are Mercator, polar, and conic.

Lessons 1-6 and 1-7

- The equator divides Earth's surface into northern and southern **hemispheres.** The distance a place is north or south of the equator is its **latitude.**
- **Meridians** are lines that run from pole to pole. The distance in degrees a place is east or west of the prime meridian is its **longitude.**
- A map's **scale** compares map distances with real distances. Map **symbols** represent real objects. The symbols are explained in a **legend.** Colors can be used to show different features.

Lesson 1-8

- Height above or below sea level is called **elevation.** The study of the form and shape of Earth's surface is called **topography.** Relief maps show elevation often using colors or shading.

Lesson 1-9

- Topographic maps use **contour lines** to show elevation. A **contour interval** is the difference in elevation between contour lines.

Key Term Challenges

atmosphere (p. 18)
contour interval (p. 34)
contour line (p. 32)
core (p. 20)
crust (p. 20)
distortion (p. 22)
Earth science (p. 16)
elevation (p. 32)
globe (p. 22)
hydrosphere (p. 18)
latitude (p. 26)
legend (p. 28)
lithosphere (p. 18)
longitude (p. 26)
mantle (p. 20)
map (p. 22)
map projection (p. 24)
meridian (p. 26)
parallel (p. 26)
scale (p. 28)
specialist (p. 16)
sphere (p. 18)
symbol (p. 28)
topography (p. 32)

MATCHING Write the Key Term from above that best matches each description.

1. layer of Earth below the crust
2. layer of gases surrounding Earth's surface
3. shows distance on a map
4. all the liquid water and ice on Earth
5. innermost region of Earth
6. flat drawing of part of Earth's surface
7. error in shape, distance, or size on a map

IDENTIFYING WORD RELATIONSHIPS Explain how the words in each pair are related. Write your answers in complete sentences.

8. contour line, elevation
9. map projection, globe
10. crust, lithosphere
11. contour interval, topography
12. latitude, parallel
13. longitude, meridian
14. symbol, legend
15. sphere, globe

Content Challenges TEST PREP

MULTIPLE CHOICE Write the letter of the term or phrase that best completes each statement.

1. The study of weather is called
   a. geology.
   b. oceanography.
   c. meteorology.
   d. specialist.

2. Earth's crust is part of the
   a. atmosphere.
   b. mantle.
   c. hydrosphere.
   d. lithosphere.

3. Rivers, lakes, and streams are part of Earth's
   a. core.
   b. mantle.
   c. hydrosphere.
   d. atmosphere.

4. The two main gases in the atmosphere are
   a. oxygen and nitrogen.
   b. oxygen and hydrogen.
   c. hydrogen and nitrogen.
   d. oxygen and helium.

5. The thickest layer of Earth is the
   a. crust.
   b. mantle.
   c. outer core.
   d. inner core.

6. Globes are
   a. two-dimensional.
   b. one-dimensional.
   c. three-dimensional.
   d. flat.

7. A map projection made by holding a sheet of paper to one pole of a globe is called a
   a. Mercator projection.
   b. polar projection.
   c. conic projection.
   d. relief projection.

8. Lines on maps or globes that run from the North Pole to the South Pole are called
   a. meridians.
   b. latitudes.
   c. longitudes.
   d. contour lines.

9. The North Pole is at
   a. 0° latitude.
   b. 10° longitude.
   c. 90° north latitude.
   d. 90° north longitude.

10. The distance in degrees east or west of the prime meridian is a place's
    a. longitude.
    b. latitude.
    c. equator.
    d. parallel.

FILL IN Write the term or phrase that best completes each statement.

11. Elevation is the distance of a point above or below _____.

12. The symbols used on a map are listed in a _____.

13. Latitude and longitude are measured in _____.

14. The longest parallel on Earth's surface is the _____.

15. A narrow field of study within a larger field is called a _____.

16. Maps of _____ areas have the fewest distortions.

17. The layer of Earth between the core and the crust is the _____.

18. The hydrosphere is the part of Earth that is _____.

Concept Challenges TEST PREP

WRITTEN RESPONSE Answer each of the following questions in complete sentences.

1. EXPLAIN: What is the longitude of Greenwich, England? Why?

2. INFER: Why must both latitude and longitude be known to find the location of a place on a map?

3. ANALYZE: Why do two contour lines never cross each other?

4. EXPLAIN: Why does a polar projection have less distortion nearer the poles than it has farther from the poles?

5. INFER: Is the diameter of Earth larger when measured from pole to pole or when measured at the equator? Explain.

INTERPRETING VISUALS Use Figure 1-34 to answer the following questions.

6. OBSERVE: What color on the map is used to show bodies of water?

7. CALCULATE: What real distance on the map is shown by 2 cm?

8. INTERPRET: How many kilometers is it from Miami, Florida, to Austin, Texas? From Charlotte, North Carolina, to Louisville, Kentucky?

9. INTERPRET: In what direction is Chicago, Illinois, from San Diego, California?

10. ANALYZE: What is the latitude and longitude of Philadelphia, Pennsylvania?

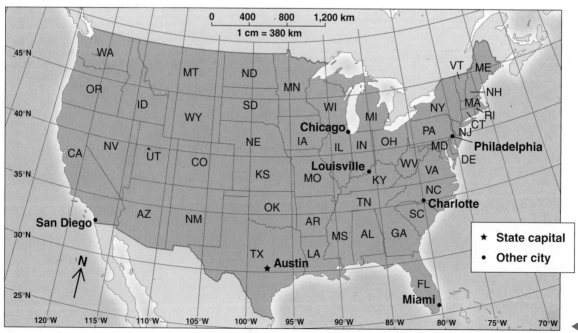

◀ Figure 1-34

Chapter 2 Minerals and Their Properties

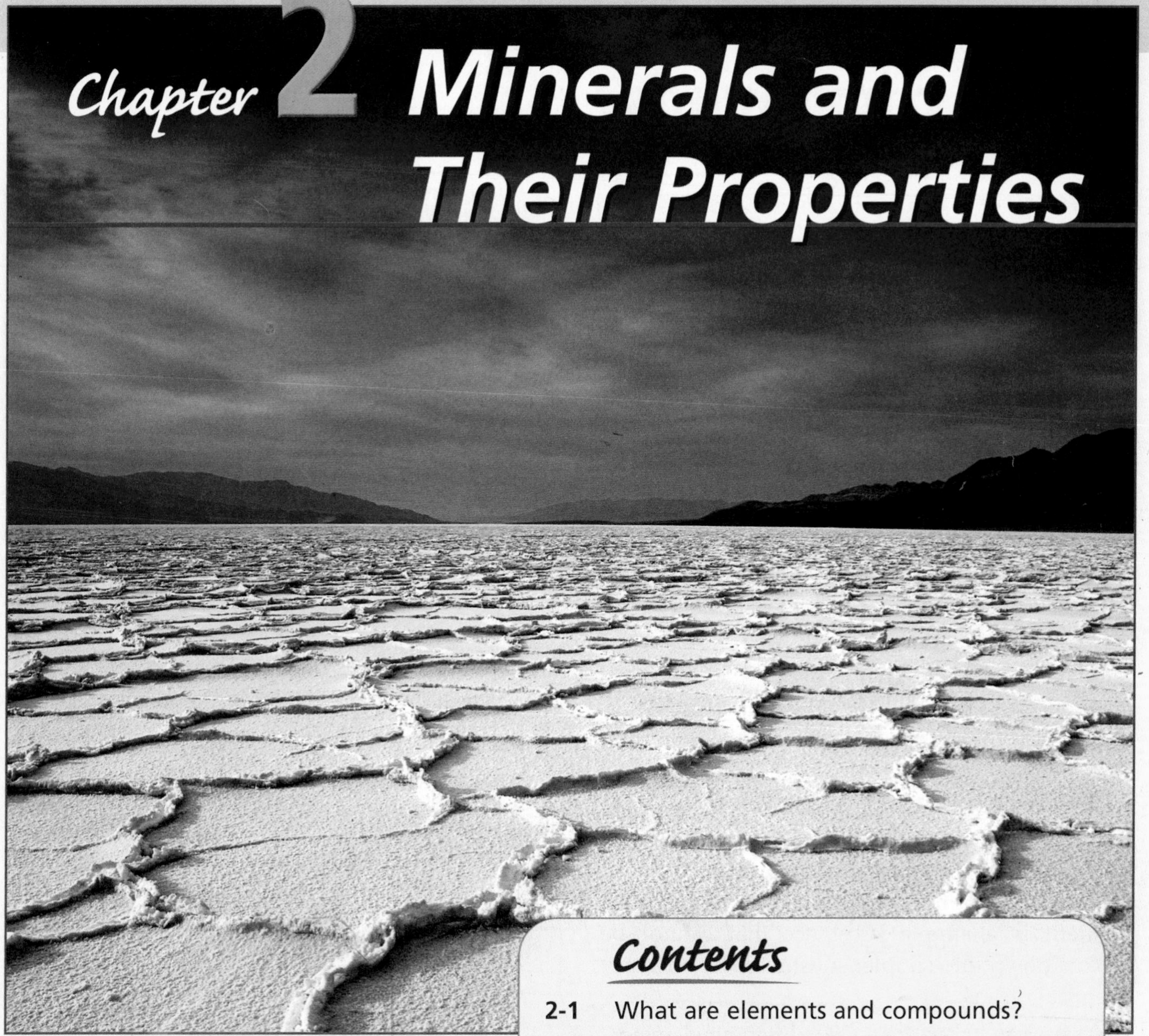

▲ **Figure 2-1** Death Valley, in southeastern California, has large salt flats.

Death Valley is a hot, dry place. Salt flats make up parts of the valley floor. Salt flats often form in pits. These pits sometimes fill with runoff from the mountain. Then, the water slowly seeps into the ground or evaporates forming salt flats. Death Valley attracts tourists and scientists because of its unusual properties.

▶Water carries dissolved minerals from the mountains to Death Valley below. What common substances do you think are left behind as the water evaporates?

Contents

2-1 What are elements and compounds?

Objectives

Define element and compound. Identify and describe some common compounds.

Key Terms

atom: smallest part of an element that can be identified as that element

element (EL-uh-muhnt): simple substance that cannot be broken down into simpler substances by ordinary chemical means

compound (KAHM-pownd): substance made up of two or more elements that are chemically combined

molecule (MAHL-ih-kyool): smallest part of a substance that has all the properties of that substance

Atoms and Elements All matter is made up of particles too small to be seen. These particles are called atoms. **Atoms** are the smallest parts of an element that can be identified as that element. An **element** is a simple substance that cannot be broken down into simpler substances by ordinary chemical means.

There are more than 100 different elements. Elements can be solids, liquids, or gases. Most elements are solids at room temperature. Only two elements, bromine and mercury, are liquid at room temperature. Oxygen, hydrogen, and nitrogen are gases. Figure 2-2 shows the states of some common elements at room temperature.

STATES OF COMMON ELEMENTS			
Element	Natural State	Element	Natural State
Carbon	Solid	Oxygen	Gas
Aluminum	Solid	Helium	Gas
Silver	Solid	Bromine	Liquid
Copper	Solid	Mercury	Liquid

▲ Figure 2-2

▲ **Figure 2-3** Mercury and copper in their natural states

▶ **1** ANALYZE: How are atoms and elements related?

Compounds Many common substances are made up of combinations of elements. Water is made up of hydrogen and oxygen. Sugar is made up of hydrogen, oxygen, and carbon. Water and sugar are examples of compounds. A **compound** is a substance made up of two or more elements that are chemically combined.

Most compounds are made up of string of atoms called **molecules.** A molecule is the smallest part of a substance that has all the chemical properties of that substance. The atoms in a molecule are chemically combined.

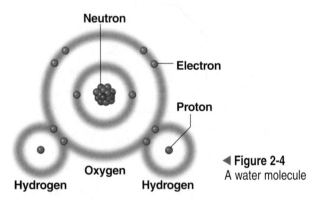

◀ **Figure 2-4**
A water molecule

▶ **2** ANALYZE: How are molecules and compounds related?

More Than Its Parts When two or more elements are combined chemically, a compound is formed. The elements in the compound are in definite proportion to each other. Most compounds have physical and chemical properties that are different from the physical and chemical properties of the elements that formed them.

Sodium is a soft metal that can be cut with a knife. Chlorine is a green gas. Both sodium and chlorine are poisonous elements. Combined, they form a solid compound that can be eaten. You know this compound, sodium chloride, as table salt.

 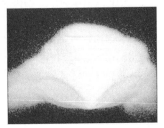

▲ **Figure 2-5** Sodium (left) is part of the compound known as table salt (right).

 IDENTIFY: What elements make up table salt?

☑ CHECKING CONCEPTS

1. About how many elements are there?
2. What form are most elements found in at room temperature?
3. What is a compound?
4. What is a molecule?

 THINKING CRITICALLY

5. **EXPLAIN:** The compound water is made from the gases oxygen and hydrogen. How is water different from the elements that make it up?
6. **ANALYZE:** How are atoms and molecules related?
7. **IDENTIFY:** What elements do the compounds sugar and water have in common?

Web InfoSearch

Alloys That Remember Alloys are metallic compounds or solutions made up of two or more elements. Some metal alloys can return to their original shape after being twisted, bent, or knotted. These are called shape memory alloys.

SEARCH: Use the Internet to find out more about alloys. What elements are they made from? What are they used for? Start your search at www.conceptsandchallenges.com. Some key search words are **shape memory alloys** and **intelligent materials.**

 How Do They Know That?

SOME ELEMENTS ARE RADIOACTIVE

A radioactive element gives off energy when particles inside its atoms break apart. Most of what is known today about radioactive elements can be traced to the work of Marie Curie and her husband, Pierre Curie.

The Curies worked with an ore called pitchblende. They observed that the pitchblende gave off unusual rays. The Curies soon discovered that these rays were being produced by two elements contained in the pitchblende. The Curies and another scientist, Henri Becquerel, shared the Nobel Prize in 1903 in physics for discovering these new elements. The elements were named polonium and radium. Polonium was named for Poland, the homeland of Marie Curie.

In 1906, Pierre Curie died in a tragic accident. However, Marie Curie continued her work with radium and polonium. In 1911, she received a second Nobel Prize, in chemistry.

Thinking Critically What do you think the energy inside an atom is used for?

▲ **Figure 2-6** Marie Curie (1867–1934) was born in Poland. However, she did her experiments in a laboratory in France.

2-2 What are chemical formulas?

Objectives

Interpret chemical symbols. Recognize common chemical formulas of some familiar compounds.

Key Terms

chemical (KEHM-ih-kuhl) **symbol:** shorthand way of writing the name of an element

chemical formula: formula that shows the elements that make up a compound

subscript (SUHB-skrihpt): number in a chemical formula that shows how many of each atom are in one molecule of a compound

Chemical Symbols

A **chemical symbol** is a shorthand way of writing the name of an element. Each element has its own chemical symbol. The chemical symbol is used to represent one atom of that element.

In 1813, a Swedish chemist named Jons Jakob Berzelius (buhr-ZEE-lee-uhs) suggested using the first letter of the name of an element as its chemical symbol. When more than one element has the same first letter, a second letter is added. That second letter is a lowercase letter.

CHEMICAL SYMBOLS			
Element	Symbol	Element	Symbol
Oxygen	O	Hydrogen	H
Nitrogen	N	Carbon	C
Aluminum	Al	Helium	He
Iron	Fe	Lead	Pb
Sodium	Na	Mercury	Hg

▲ Figure 2-7

Some elements do not use the first letters of their English names as their symbols. The symbols for these elements may come from the names of the elements in a different language.

Look at Figure 2-7 for some examples. The chemical symbol for sodium is Na. This comes from the Latin name for sodium, which is *natrium.*

▶ **IDENTIFY:** Why do some elements have unusual letters for their symbols?

Chemical Formulas We just learned that a chemical symbol is a shorthand way of writing the name of an element. Chemical symbols are most often used to write chemical formulas. A **chemical formula** shows the elements that make up a compound. Sodium chloride is the chemical name for table salt. The chemical formula for sodium chloride is NaCl. By looking at the formula, you can see that table salt is made up of sodium and chlorine. The chemical symbol for sodium is Na. For chlorine, it is Cl.

▶ **2 ANALYZE:** How are chemical symbols and chemical formulas related?

Subscripts Hydrogen peroxide is a compound made from hydrogen (H) and oxygen (O). The chemical formula for hydrogen peroxide is H_2O_2.

The number 2 after the H and the O is called a **subscript.** Subscripts show how many of each atom are in a molecule of a compound. Subscripts are written slightly below the line.

The chemical formulas for some compounds are shown in Figure 2-8. The chemical formula for the compound iron sulfide is FeS_2. This chemical formula shows that a molecule of this compound contains two atoms of sulfur (S) and one atom of iron. When there is no subscript, it means that there is only one atom of that element in the molecule.

CHEMICAL FORMULAS FOR COMMON COMPOUNDS	
Compound	Formula
Water	H_2O
Carbon monoxide	CO
Carbon dioxide	CO_2
Iron sulfide	FeS_2
Calcium carbonate	$CaCO_3$
Aluminum oxide	Al_2O_3
Ammonium hydroxide	NH_4OH
Silica	SiO_2
Sodium phosphate	$NaPO_4$
Hydrogen peroxide	H_2O_2

▲ Figure 2-8

▲ **Figure 2-9** The chemical compound iron sulfide (FeS$_2$), also known as pyrite, has two atoms of sulfur in each molecule.

3 ▶ **INTERPRET:** What do subscripts show?

✔ CHECKING CONCEPTS

1. Chemical symbols are shorthand for _____.

2. Subscripts are written slightly _____ the line.

3. A chemical symbol stands for one _____ of an element.

4. The first letter of a chemical symbol is always a _____ letter.

💡 THINKING CRITICALLY

5. **ANALYZE:** Why do you think scientists need shorthand ways of writing elements and compounds?

INTERPRETING VISUALS

Use Figure 2-8 to answer the following questions.

6. **CALCULATE:** How many atoms make up one molecule of carbon dioxide?

7. **ANALYZE:** How does a molecule of carbon monoxide differ from a molecule of carbon dioxide?

8. **IDENTIFY:** How many different elements are in calcium carbonate?

Hands-On Activity

INTERPRETING CHEMICAL FORMULAS

1. Copy the table in Figure 2-10 onto a clean sheet of paper.

2. On your paper, fill in the information that is missing from the table. Use the tables from this lesson and Lesson 2-1 to help you identify the elements in each compound.

Practicing Your Skills

3. **EXPLAIN:** What information does a chemical formula contain?

4. **COMPARE/CONTRAST:** How does the chemical formula for aluminum oxide differ from the chemical formula for aluminum sulfide?

5. **INFER:** Why do scientists use chemical formulas?

CHEMICAL FORMULAS AND THEIR MEANING			
Chemical Formula	Name of Compound	Elements in Compound	Relative Numbers of Atoms in Compound
H$_2$O	Water	Hydrogen and oxygen	2 atoms of hydrogen for every 1 atom of oxygen
CO$_2$	Carbon dioxide	Carbon and oxygen	1 atom of carbon for every 2 atoms of oxygen
CO	Carbon monoxide		
NaCl	Sodium chloride		
Al$_2$O$_3$	Aluminum oxide		
Al$_2$S$_3$	Aluminum sulfide		
H$_2$SO$_4$	Sulfuric acid		

▲ **Figure 2-10**

2-3 What are minerals?

Objectives

Define mineral. Identify and describe some minerals found in Earth's crust.

Key Term

mineral (MIHN-uhr-uhl): naturally occurring, inorganic solid formed from elements or compounds and having a definite chemical makeup and regular atomic structure

Earth's Crust The crust is the outer layer of Earth. It is made up of large chunks of solid rock and smaller pieces of rock, sand particles, and soil. Sand and soil are rock that has been broken into small pieces. All materials in Earth's crust are made up of elements and compounds.

About 75 percent of Earth's crust is made up of the elements oxygen and silicon. When oxygen and silicon combine, silica is formed. Sand is composed mostly of silica in the form of quartz.

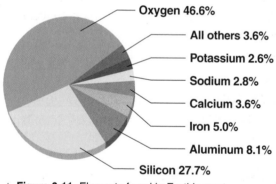

- Oxygen 46.6%
- All others 3.6%
- Potassium 2.6%
- Sodium 2.8%
- Calcium 3.6%
- Iron 5.0%
- Aluminum 8.1%
- Silicon 27.7%

▲ **Figure 2-11** Elements found in Earth's crust

Look at Figure 2-11 above. It shows the elements that make up most of Earth's crust. It also shows what percentage of Earth's crust is made up of each element. These elements are found combined into many different compounds.

▶ **DESCRIBE:** What does Earth's crust consist of?

Natural Solids A **mineral** is a naturally occurring solid. It is formed from elements or compounds in Earth's crust. All minerals are inorganic. This means that they are not formed from living things or from the remains of living things.

A mineral may be either an element or a compound. Each mineral has a definite chemical makeup. Gold and silver are examples of minerals that are made up of only one element. Mostly, however, minerals are combinations of elements. For example, the mineral quartz is a compound. Quartz is made up of silicon and oxygen. The chemical formulas for some commonly found minerals are shown in Figure 2-12.

SOME MINERALS AND THEIR CHEMICAL FORMULAS			
Mineral	**Formula**	**Mineral**	**Formula**
Gold	Au	Calcite	$CaCO_3$
Silver	Ag	Halite	NaCl
Copper	Cu	Galena	PbS
Quartz	SiO_2	Pyrite	FeS_2

▲ **Figure 2-12**

2 **INTERPRET:** What are the elements that make up halite?

Rock-Forming Minerals The rocks that make up Earth's crust are made up of minerals. Scientists have identified more than 2,000 minerals. However, fewer than 20 of these minerals are commonly found in Earth's crust. These common minerals are called rock-forming minerals. Most rock-forming minerals are compounds.

▲ **Figure 2-13** Sand is made up mostly of silicon and oxygen. Silicon makes up a large part of Earth's crust.

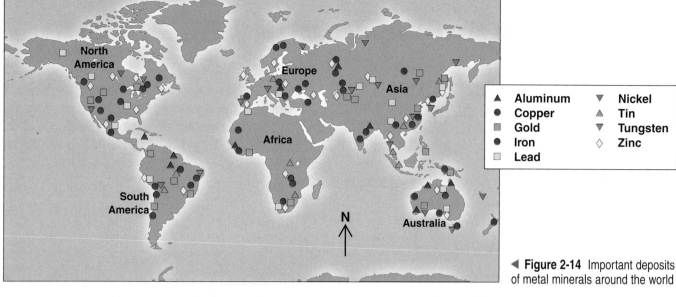

 Figure 2-14 Important deposits of metal minerals around the world

In a rock, the minerals are usually found as mixtures. In a mixture, two or more substances come together. However, the substances do not chemically combine. They retain their original properties. In the case of rocks, each mineral retains its color, texture, and chemical makeup.

3 EXPLAIN: Why are rocks called mixtures?

Metal Minerals Minerals that can be recovered for use are called mineral resources. Aluminum, iron, copper, and silver are some metal minerals. Metals are useful because they can be stretched into wire, flattened into sheets, and hammered or molded without breaking. Tools, machinery, and even the steel girders used in buildings were all made of materials inside Earth's crust. Metals can be found in many places around the world. See Figure 2-14 for some examples.

4 NAME: What are some metal minerals?

☑ CHECKING CONCEPTS

1. About three-fourths of Earth's crust is made up of oxygen and _____ .
2. Quartz is made up mostly of _____ .
3. Calcite has _____ atom of calcium for every three atoms of oxygen.
4. Gold is both an element and a _____ .

💡 THINKING CRITICALLY

Use Figure 2-11 to answer questions 5 through 8.

5. OBSERVE: Which element makes up almost half of Earth's crust?
6. IDENTIFY: What are two elements of Earth's crust that are found in only small amounts?
7. CALCULATE: What percentage of Earth's crust is made up of iron?
8. SEQUENCE: What five elements make up most of Earth's crust, from most common to least?
9. INTERPRET: What two ways does the map legend in Figure 2-14 use to show metal mineral resources?
10. INTERPRET: Based on Figure 2-14, what is the most abundant metal mineral found around the world?

BUILDING SCIENCE SKILLS

Organizing a Collection There are more than 2,000 different minerals. However, you are likely to find less than 100 of these. You can buy specimens from museums and rock and mineral shows. Or, you can look for your own minerals on mountains, in rock quarries, or at the beach. All you need is goggles, a hammer, a chisel or a geologist's pick, and a collecting sack. Record the date, location, and name of any mineral you find. Use a field guide to help you identify it. Put your samples in labeled boxes. ⚠ CAUTION: Do not trespass on private land. Also, be aware that some national parks and beaches do not permit the taking of minerals.

2-4 How do we identify minerals?

Objective
Describe the properties that can be used to identify minerals.

Key Terms
physical property: observable characteristic that describes an object

streak: color of the powder left by a mineral

luster: how a mineral's surface reflects light

hardness: property of a mineral that relates to how much the mineral resists being scratched

Physical Properties The characteristics of an object that can be observed or measured are its **physical properties.** The element iron is gray. Objects made out of iron are attracted to a magnet. These are two physical properties of iron. Physical properties can be used to help identify minerals. Some physical properties of minerals are color, streak, luster, and hardness.

▶ **1** LIST: What are some physical properties of minerals?

Color and Streak Color is an important property of minerals. However, most minerals cannot be identified by color alone. Many minerals are the same color. Gold and pyrite are both brassy yellow. Other minerals are found in more than one color. Quartz, for example, can be purple, yellow, pink, or colorless. It may also be brown, black, or white. Two minerals that are found only in a single color are malachite and azurite. Malachite is always green. Azurite is always blue.

▲ Figure 2-15 Malachite is a green mineral.

Streak is the color of the powder left by a mineral. You can find the streak of a mineral by rubbing the mineral across a square of unglazed ceramic tile. A mineral may be found in many different colors. Its streak, however, is always the same color.

Chalk is made up of the mineral calcite. When you write with a piece of naturally occurring chalk, the calcite leaves a white powder that you can see.

▲ Figure 2-16 Streaks of powder are made by scratching two forms of the mineral hematite on an unglazed ceramic tile.

▶ **2** DESCRIBE: What is the streak of calcite?

Luster The way a mineral's surface reflects light is called **luster.** A mineral can have either a metallic or a nonmetallic luster. Minerals with a metallic luster shine like new coins. Other minerals may look waxy, glassy, or dull. Quartz has a glassy luster. Calcite has a glassy or a dull luster.

▲ Figure 2-17 Silver (left) is a metal valued for its high luster, among other properties. Fluorite has a dull, waxy, or glassy luster.

▶ **3** IDENTIFY: What are two kinds of luster?

Hardness The property of a mineral that relates to how much it resists being scratched is called **hardness.** In 1812, Friedrich Mohs, an Austrian mineralogist, worked out a scale of hardness for minerals.

Mohs' scale ranks ten minerals in hardness from 1 to 10. As the numbers increase, the hardness of the minerals also increases. A mineral with a high number can scratch any mineral that has a lower number. However, a mineral with a lower number cannot scratch a mineral that has a higher number.

MOHS' SCALE OF HARDNESS			
Mineral	Hardness	Mineral	Hardness
Talc	1	Orthoclase	6
Gypsum	2	Quartz	7
Calcite	3	Topaz	8
Fluorite	4	Corundum	9
Apatite	5	Diamond	10

▲ **Figure 2-18**

 ANALYZE: What mineral is the hardest on Mohs' scale?

✓ CHECKING CONCEPTS

1. What property allows one mineral to scratch another?
2. What is luster?
3. How is the streak of a mineral found?

THINKING CRITICALLY

4. **IDENTIFY:** What are some physical properties of the mineral diamond?
5. **INFER:** Why is streak a better way to identify a mineral than color is?

DESIGNING AN EXPERIMENT

Design an experiment to solve the following problem. Include a hypothesis, variables, a procedure with materials, and the type of data to study. Be sure to say how you will record your data.

PROBLEM: Joan had two blue minerals. One left a blue streak. The other left a white streak. What other tests could Joan do to identify the minerals?

Hands-On Activity

PERFORMING HARDNESS TESTS

You will need a penny, a butter knife, a piece of glass, and an iron nail.

1. A field hardness scale, like the one in Figure 2-19, can help you determine a mineral's hardness. If a mineral scratches glass, it is harder than glass. If glass scratches the mineral, the mineral is softer than glass.

2. First, try to scratch the glass with your fingernail. ⚠ CAUTION: Do *not* scratch your fingernail with the glass.

FIELD HARDNESS SCALE	
Hardness	Test
1	Scratched easily with fingernail
2	Scratched by fingernail (2.5)
3	Scratched by a penny
4	Scratched easily by a butter knife; does not scratch glass
5	Hard to scratch with a butter knife; barely scratches glass (5.5)
6	Scratched by an iron nail (6.5); easily scratches glass
7	Scratches an iron nail and glass

▲ **Figure 2-19**

3. To find the hardest material, try scratching each material mentioned with the others. Look carefully where you scratched. Are there any marks?

Practicing Your Skills

4. **SEQUENCE:** List the objects in order from hardest to softest.
5. **IDENTIFY:** Which material will scratch all of the others?
6. **CONCLUDE:** How can you find the hardness of a mineral using the materials mentioned?

2-5 What are some other ways to identify minerals?

INVESTIGATE

Testing for Calcium Carbonate
HANDS-ON ACTIVITY

1. Obtain a sample of calcite or limestone and a sample of granite.

2. Put on goggles and a lab apron. Use an eyedropper to place a few drops of weak hydrochloric acid on each sample. Observe and record what happens to each.
   ⚠ CAUTION: Acids can cause serious burns.

3. Rinse both samples under warm running water and wash your hands.

THINK ABOUT IT: Coral has a similar chemical composition to limestone. How do you think it would react to the acid?

STEP 2

Objective

Explain how density, magnetism, and an acid test can be used to identify minerals.

Key Terms

density (DEHN-suh-tee)**:** amount of matter in a given volume

magnetism (MAG-nuh-tihz-uhm)**:** force of attraction or repulsion associated with magnets

acid test: test that helps identify minerals containing calcium carbonate

Density All matter has mass and volume. **Density** is the amount of matter in a given volume. You can calculate the density of an object by using the following formula:

$$\text{Density} = \text{Mass} \div \text{Volume}$$

As an example, suppose that you have a sample of the mineral talc. Your sample has a mass of 26 g and a volume of 10 cm^3. If you divide 26 g by 10 cm^3, you will get a density of 2.6 g/cm^3.

▲ **Figure 2-20** Talc is a soft, light mineral.

Density is a property of minerals that never changes. For this reason, density can be used to help identify minerals. Density is measured in grams per cubic centimeter, or g/cm^3. Most minerals have a density that measures between 2 and 3 g/cm^3.

▶ 1 EXPLAIN: How can density be used to identify minerals?

Magnetism **Magnetism** is a force of attraction or repulsion shown by matter that is magnetic. Magnetism is displayed when objects made of iron, nickel, or cobalt are attracted to a magnet. Steel, which is an alloy of iron, also shows magnetism. Magnetite is a mineral that contains iron. If you held a small chunk of magnetite near a magnet, the magnetite would be attracted to the magnet. Magnetite can also sometimes act as a magnet itself. Magnetite shows the property of magnetism.

▲ **Figure 2-21** Magnetite is also called lodestone. This mineral attracts the steel in paper clips.

▶ 2 EXPLAIN: How could you use a magnet to determine if an unknown mineral is magnetite?

The Acid Test Some minerals contain calcium carbonate ($CaCO_3$). Knowing that a mineral contains this compound can help you identify the mineral. To test for calcium carbonate in a mineral, you place a drop of a weak acid on a small piece of the mineral, as you did in the activity at the start of this lesson. If the surface of the mineral fizzes, the mineral contains calcium carbonate. This is the **acid test.** Calcite and dolomite are two minerals that contain calcium carbonate.

 EXPLAIN: What is the acid test?

 CHECKING CONCEPTS

1. What is density?
2. Which common mineral is attracted to a magnet?
3. What kinds of minerals can be identified by the acid test?

 THINKING CRITICALLY

4. **IDENTIFY:** What two properties must be known to calculate the density of a mineral?
5. **CALCULATE:** What is the density of an object with a mass of 49 g and a volume of 7 cm^3?
6. **ANALYZE:** How can the property of magnetism be used to help you identify two gray minerals?

DESIGNING AN EXPERIMENT

Design an experiment to solve the following problem. Include a hypothesis, variables, a procedure, and the type of data to study. List the materials you need, and tell how you would record your data.

PROBLEM: How can the minerals quartz and calcite be identified?

Integrating Physical Science

TOPICS: metallic elements, density

FINDING THE DENSITY OF GOLD

Pure gold scratches easily. It is often mixed with silver or copper to make it harder. Jewelers measure the purity of gold in carats, or parts per 24. Twenty-four-carat gold is pure gold. Fourteen-carat gold is 14/24 pure, or 58 percent gold.

Have you ever wondered whether a piece of yellow, shiny jewelry was really gold? Color and luster are important properties of minerals. However, other properties must be identified for gold to be considered genuine.

In ancient times, a king asked a goldsmith to make him a 1-kg crown of gold. The goldsmith replaced some of the gold with silver. The goldsmith then made the king a crown with a mass of 1 kg.

▲ Figure 2-22
Archimedes (above) may have tested a crown similar to the one shown here.

The king thought the goldsmith had stolen some of the gold but could not prove it. He asked Archimedes, a scientist and mathematician, for help. Archimedes calculated the density of the crown. He compared it with the density of gold. They were different. The crown was not pure gold. The goldsmith had stolen some of the King's gold.

Thinking Critically What are some properties of gold other than color and luster?

2-6 What are crystals, cleavage, and fracture?

Objectives
Define crystals and show how they are related to minerals. Distinguish between fracture and cleavage in minerals.

Key Terms
crystal (KRIHS-tuhl): solid substance with its atoms arranged in a regular three-dimensional pattern

cleavage (KLEEV-ihj): tendency of some minerals to split along smooth, flat surfaces called planes

fracture (FRAK-chuhr): tendency of some minerals to break into pieces with uneven surfaces

Crystal Shapes All minerals are made up of crystals. A **crystal** is a solid material in which the atoms are arranged in a regular pattern. This pattern is repeated over and over in a regular internal structure. This structure determines the external shape of the crystal. The crystals that make up a given mineral always have the same shape, but they may differ in size.

Crystal shape is a property of minerals. There are six basic crystal systems that describe crystal structure. Scientists use X-rays to study the structures of crystals. They can use the structure of a crystal to help identify the mineral.

▶ **DEFINE:** What is a crystal?

Cleavage Cleavage is a property of some minerals. **Cleavage** is the tendency of a mineral to split along smooth, flat surfaces called planes. Mica is a mineral that splits into flat sheets. Mica looks like layers of thin plastic.

Different minerals have different kinds of cleavage. However, the way the mineral splits, or shows cleavage, is always the same for that mineral. Mica cleaves into thin, flat sheets. Galena splits into small cubes. Feldspar shows what is called steplike cleavage.

▲ **Figure 2-24** Mica (Top) and feldspar (bottom)

▶ **DEFINE:** What is cleavage in minerals?

Fracture A mineral shows **fracture** when it breaks into pieces with uneven surfaces. The fracture may be even, uneven, hackly, or concoidal. Hackly minerals have sharp, jagged surfaces. Copper shows a hackly structure. Concoidal minerals have ringed ridges or indentations like those of seashells. Obsidian shows concoidal

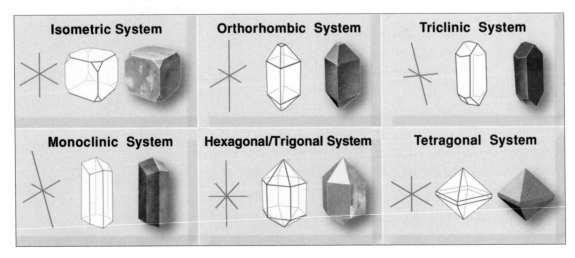

| Isometric System | Orthorhombic System | Triclinic System |
| Monoclinic System | Hexagonal/Trigonal System | Tetragonal System |

◀ **Figure 2-23**
The six basic crystal systems

fracture. Some minerals break into splinters or fibers. One example of this is asbestos.

HOW MINERALS BREAK APART

Cleavage	Examples	Fracture	Examples
Pieces with smooth, flat surfaces	Mica, galena, feldspar	Pieces with rough, jagged, or uneven surfaces	Copper, obsidian, asbestos

▲ Figure 2-25

 CONTRAST: How are fracture and cleavage different?

 CHECKING CONCEPTS

1. How do scientists study crystal structure?
2. What kind of cleavage does mica show?
3. What is fracture?
4. What do the surfaces of a mineral with fracture look like?

 THINKING CRITICALLY

5. **MODEL:** Halite forms cubic crystals. Draw the crystal form of a piece of halite.
6. **IDENTIFY:** Steplike cleavage is a property of what mineral?
7. **INFER:** What property of minerals splits the mineral into pieces with uneven surfaces?
8. **DESCRIBE:** How does galena look when split?

BUILDING SCIENCE SKILLS

Classifying Minerals have either cleavage or fracture. Find out whether each mineral listed shows cleavage or fracture. Then, make a chart listing each mineral in the appropriate box.

pyroxene	quartz
anatase	corundum
periclase	calcite
amphibole	opal
brookite	hematite
thorianite	talc

People in Science

GEMSTONE CUTTER

A gemstone cutter works with beautiful and valuable minerals called gems. The gem cutter may take the gemstone, such as a diamond, as it is found in nature and split it into two or three parts. Then, a grinding wheel and other tools are used to polish the dull stone. This creates flat surfaces called facets (FAS-ihts) that make the stone sparkle.

Most gem cutters cut gems for jewelry. Some create sculptures. Lawrence Stoller is a gem artist. He was taught gem-cutting by Glenn Lehrer. Stoller and Lehrer together developed many of the tools and technologies used to cut large stones.

Stoller has cut many of the world's largest gemstones. He is best known for his giant sculpted crystals. Some of these are in museums. Stoller also cuts tools for physicists and surgeons.

Gemstone cutting requires skill, focus, and patience. A mistake can destroy a costly stone. Most gem cutters learn their trade on the job.

Thinking Critically If you were to do gem cutting as a hobby, why would you use stones such as agate and quartz?

▲ Figure 2-26 Gemstone cutters use grinding wheels to polish gemstones.

How are minerals formed?

INVESTIGATE

Forming Crystals Fast and Slow
HANDS-ON ACTIVITY

STEP 1

1. Put on safety goggles and gloves. Using tweezers or a spoon, put a small amount of baking soda on each of two microscope slides. Carefully place the slides on a hot plate set on low. ⚠ CAUTION: Be careful when using a hot plate.

2. When the baking soda melts, carefully move one slide aside with tweezers and put it on a paper towel to cool. Place the second slide on some ice cubes.

3. When the baking soda on both slides is hard, examine the slide using a hand lens or a microscope.

THINK ABOUT IT: How are the crystals on the two slides different?

Objective
Describe the main ways minerals are formed.

Key Terms
crystallization: formation of crystals caused by processes such as cooling and evaporation

evaporation (ee-vap-uh-RAY-shuhn)**:** process by which a liquid changes into a gas

solution: mixture in which the particles of one substance are evenly mixed with the particles of another substance

precipitation (pree-sihp-uh-TAY-shuhn)**:** process that occurs when elements and compounds leave a solution and crystallize out as solids

Minerals in the Crust Earth's crust is made up of rocks. Rocks, in turn, are made up of minerals. Most minerals are compounds in crystal form. In some rocks, the crystals are very large and easy to identify. In other rocks, the crystals are very tiny.

▶ **RELATE:** How are minerals and rocks related?

Magma Cooling Molten rock, or magma, is a very hot mixture of many different minerals. Magma is found in deep underground chambers. As long as the magma stays hot, it remains liquid. Eventually, though, the magma cools. If it cools slowly underground, large mineral crystals start forming. This is called **crystallization.** Eventually, the mineral crystals grow together to form rock.

Sometimes, cracks form in the rock above magma chambers. Pressure causes the magma to move up to the surface. When it comes out, the magma, now called lava, cools more quickly than it would have underground. Soon, the lava hardens into rock that contains small crystals.

▶ **CONTRAST:** How do crystals that cool very slowly differ from crystals that cool rapidly?

Evaporation The second way minerals form is by **evaporation.** In this process, water evaporates, or changes to a gas. The water in lakes and oceans contains dissolved minerals. As the water evaporates, only the mineral crystals remain. The crystals grow together to form rock.

▶ **IDENTIFY:** How do crystals form from evaporated water?

Precipitation Sometimes the elements in a mineral dissolve in water heated by magma. These dissolved minerals form solutions. A **solution** is a mixture in which the particles of one substance are evenly mixed with the particles of another substance. When the solution begins to cool, the elements and compounds leave the solution and crystallize out as solids. This process is **precipitation.**

Crystals can also form when water has more dissolved minerals than it can usually hold. For example, warm water can dissolve more halite (salt) than cold water can. The Great Salt Lake of Utah has very salty water. A very hot and dry climate causes evaporation and salt to crystallize out.

Many minerals form where there are cracks in the ocean floor. First, ocean water seeps down through the cracks. The water is heated by magma in the crust. The heated water dissolves the minerals in the crust. This hot solution is released through vents called chimneys as shown in Figure 2-27. When the hot solution hits cold seawater, minerals crystallize out and then fall to the ocean floor.

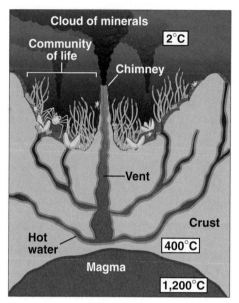

Cloud of minerals
Community of life
2°C
Chimney
Vent
Crust
Hot water
400°C
Magma
1,200°C

◀ **Figure 2-27**
A deep-sea vent is a crack in the ocean floor.

▶ 4 DESCRIBE: What are chimneys?

✓ CHECKING CONCEPTS

1. What are minerals?
2. What causes big crystals to form?
3. What causes tiny crystals to form?
4. What happens as water containing dissolved minerals evaporates from lakes and oceans?

💡 THINKING CRITICALLY

5. **INFER:** What black, glassy mineral might you get if molten lava cooled so rapidly that crystals did not have time to form?
6. **INFER:** Sometimes rock has both large and small mineral crystals. How can you explain this?

BUILDING SCIENCE SKILLS

Classifying Find out what is meant by the following terms: *silicates, carbonates, sulfates, halides,* and *oxides.* Write a definition for each term. Then, find examples of two minerals that can be put into each group.

Integrating Life Science

TOPICS: medicine, health

PROTEIN CRYSTALS
The human body contains more than 100,000 different proteins. Proteins perform many important functions. For example, they allow muscles to contract. They help your bones grow and form the attachments for muscles. They also help fight diseases.

Proteins are made up of very complex molecules. These molecules are strung out like long, twisted ribbons. Scientists can crystallize the proteins and analyze the molecules. However, Earth's gravity distorts the crystals as they form.

In flight, the space shuttle acts as a gravity-free environment. Scientists have performed protein crystal experiments on the shuttle. This has allowed them to grow large protein crystals that are not distorted by gravity. These crystals may be effective at fighting diseases such as cancer.

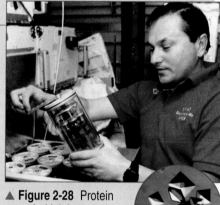

▲ **Figure 2-28** Protein crystals (right) grown in space by Russian cosmonaut Vladimir G. Titan (above)

Thinking Critically The space shuttle can only remain in space for a few weeks. The International Space Station (ISS) will have a permanent orbiting laboratory. Would the ISS be better for growing crystals? Why or why not?

LAB ACTIVITY
Growing a Crystal Garden

Materials

Goggles, lab apron, sugar, salt, magnesium sulfate (Epsom salts), food coloring, hot water, plastic cups, plastic foam egg carton, scissors, tablespoon, ballpoint pen, magnifying glass

BACKGROUND

Most rocks contain minerals in crystal form. A crystal has a regular geometric shape, such as a cube. Some minerals form under water. Minerals, dissolved in the water, can crystallize out as the water evaporates or cools. Eventually, the crystals grow together and become minerals or rocks.

PURPOSE

In this activity, you will dissolve minerals in water to form solutions. As the solutions evaporate, the minerals will recrystallize.

PROCEDURE

1. Cut the egg carton so that you have three egg cups joined together. Leave a little of the carton lid above the hinge to write your name.
   ⚠ **CAUTION:** Be careful when using scissors.

2. Put on your safety goggles and lab apron.

3. Look at the crystal recipes listed in Figure 2-29. Place the right amount of ingredients for the first recipe in one of the plastic cups.

4. Add the right amount of hot water to the cup. Stir until all the chemicals dissolve.
   ⚠ **CAUTION:** Be careful when using hot water.

5. Add food coloring to the solution and stir.

6. Pour one tablespoon of your crystal solution into one egg cup. Share the rest of your solution with others doing the experiment.

▲ **STEP 1** Cut the egg carton to form three cups.

▲ **STEP 4** Stir until all chemicals are dissolved.

56 ◆ E

7. Mix and pour the other crystal solutions into the other cups. Do not touch the egg cups for one week unless instructed to do so by your teacher.

8. One week later, carefully pour any remaining crystal solutions in your egg cups into the sink. Let the crystals dry.

9. Examine the crystals with a magnifying glass. Record your observations in a notebook.

▲ **STEP 7** Pour one tablespoon of each crystal solution into an egg cup.

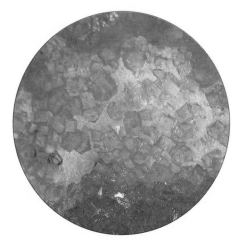

◀ **STEP 9** Examine the crystals with a magnifying glass.

Crystal Recipes

Halite (salt)	Sugar	Epsom salts
5 tbs salt	5 tbs sugar	5 tbs Epsom salts
6 tbs hot water	5 tbs hot water	5 tbs hot water
Green food coloring	Red food coloring	Blue food coloring

▲ **Figure 2-29** Use these recipes to make your crystal solutions.

CONCLUSIONS

1. **OBSERVE:** What do you see?

2. **OBSERVE:** What are the shapes of the crystals?

3. **ANALYZE:** Why are the crystals attached to each other?

4. **INFER:** How do your results resemble the way some kinds of rocks form at the bottom of the ocean?

2-8 How are minerals used?

Objective
State some common uses of minerals.

Key Terms
ore: mineral that is mined because it contains useful metals or nonmetals

gem: stone that has been cut and polished

Mineral Uses Many products are made from minerals. Diamond crystals are used to make jewelry. Because they are so hard, diamonds are also used to make cutting and drilling tools.

Gypsum is a mineral that is commonly used to make plaster. Many walls and ceilings are made of plaster. Some minerals and their uses are shown in Figure 2-30.

MINERALS AND THEIR USES	
Mineral	**Uses**
Quartz	Glass, sandpaper, telephone, radio
Feldspar	Porcelain, china, dishes
Mica	Insulators, toasters, irons, motors
Talc	Talcum powder, crayons, soap
Calcite	Building materials, medicine
Graphite	Pencil lead

▲ Figure 2-30

Tiny amounts of minerals are needed as part of your diet to keep your body healthy and working properly. Calcium and phosphorus are two examples of minerals needed by your body. These minerals are needed for strong bones and teeth. The body uses the mineral iron to make new red blood cells.

The minerals your body needs are found in food substances. Calcium, for example, is found in milk and other dairy products. Iron is found in red meat and some vegetables. The minerals that are used in dietary supplements are usually found in compounds.

▶ **IDENTIFY:** What are two minerals used by the human body?

Ores Minerals in the form of compounds contain useful metals and nonmetals. An **ore** is a rocky material that is mined because it contains useful metals or nonmetals that can be extracted from it.

Some examples of ores are hematite, bauxite, and halite. Hematite contains iron, which is used in the production of steel. Bauxite is mined to extract aluminum. Halite contains salt.

▲ **Figure 2-31** Hematite iron ore

▶ **DEFINE:** What is an ore?

Gemstones and Gems Some minerals are valued because they are beautiful and long lasting. These minerals are called gemstones. Rare and beautiful gemstones are called precious stones. Gemstones that are more common are called semiprecious stones. Because they are beautiful and long lasting, many precious and semiprecious stones are used to make jewelry.

▲ **Figure 2-32** Ruby (left) from corundum and emerald (right) from beryl are both precious stones used in making jewelry.

Gemstones that have been cut and polished are called **gems**. Diamonds, rubies, sapphires, and emeralds are precious stones that are often made into gems. Opal, amethyst, turquoise, topaz, garnet, aquamarine, and jade are some semiprecious stones that are made into gems.

▲ **Figure 2-33** Opal (above) and turquoise (left) are both semiprecious stones used in making jewelry.

 IDENTIFY: What are three precious stones?

☑ **CHECKING CONCEPTS**

1. Calcium and _____ are both needed by the body for strong bones and teeth.
2. Bauxite is an _____ of aluminum.
3. Plaster is made from _____ .
4. Very rare and beautiful minerals are called _____ stones.
5. Halite is an ore of _____.

💡 **THINKING CRITICALLY**

6. LIST: What are four minerals that are commonly taken from ores?

INTERPRETING VISUALS

Use Figure 2-30 to answer the following questions.

7. LIST: Which minerals are used to make items found in the bathroom?
8. IDENTIFY: What is the most common use of graphite?
9. IDENTIFY: Which mineral do objects that require heat insulation usually contain?

Science and Technology

GEMS FROM THE LABORATORY

Precious stones are rare. They are prized for their color, luster, and hardness. Any combination of these properties makes a precious stone desirable and costly.

Many gems are now made in laboratories. For example, crystals of quartz are heated until they change color. They are then sold as topaz. Such stones are called treated gems. A three-piece sandwich of heat-treated aquamarine inside of green glass can be substituted for an emerald. This is an example of an assembled gem.

Corundum is the second hardest of all minerals. It can be specially treated to form synthetic rubies and sapphires. These look just like the naturally occurring gemstones.

▲ **Figure 2-34** Synthetic gems, which are made in laboratories, can be very difficult to tell from natural gems. Above are synthetic rubies.

Thinking Critically Manufactured gems are hard to tell from the real thing. Should they be as costly as the natural gems they resemble?

THE Big IDEA

How can the element carbon form different substances?

How are a lump of coal, the point of a pencil, and a sparkling diamond alike? All three substances are made up mostly of carbon atoms. However, the carbon atoms are arranged in different ways.

Coal is a carbon-rich organic material. It took millions of years to form. Overgrown swamps once covered huge areas of land, and the climate was mild and rainy. As the plants died, they became buried. Pressure and heat caused the deep deposits of buried plants to change into coal.

Graphite is a mineral made up entirely of carbon. The atoms in graphite are arranged in sheets. They are held together by weak chemical bonds. When these bonds break, as they do under light pressure, some of the carbon atoms flake off. That is why graphite is often used in pencils. Pressing on the pencil leaves behind a trail of carbon. Graphite is also used to lubricate machines.

Diamond is also a mineral made up entirely of carbon atoms. However, the diamonds crystallize only under extreme pressure. In nature, they are created by geological processes deep within Earth. Other processes, such as the wearing away of surface rock, bring the diamonds to the surface.

The atoms that make up diamonds are tightly bonded together. Its internal crystal structure makes diamond the hardest natural substance known.

Look at the illustrations on these two pages. Then, follow the directions in the Science Log to learn more about "the big idea." ✦

Coal Swamp

Coal is not a mineral but an organic material. It is formed from the remains of living things, mostly plants. Most coal was formed in huge, overgrown swamps during the Carboniferous Period, 300 to 350 million years ago.

WRITING ACTIVITY

Science Log

Imagine that you are a scientist exploring how carbon atoms combine to form different substances. Your research team gets on board a special vehicle that can travel through solids such as coal, graphite, and diamond. Write a few paragraphs describing your observations. Start your search at www.conceptsandchallenges.com.

Anthracite

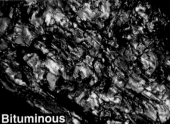
Bituminous

Lignite

Types of Coal

Coal forms from the remains of living things. It is not a mineral and does not have a regular atomic structure. Coal is classified according to the amount of carbon it contains. Anthracite (hard) coal is made up mostly of carbon. It is found in rocks that are more than 65 million years old. There is also bituminous coal and lignite, which are softer forms of coal and contain more impurities such as sulfer.

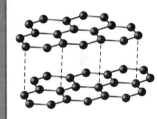

Graphite

Graphite is made up of layers of carbon. The layers are loosely bonded to each other. This internal crystal structure makes graphite a very soft substance.

Diamond

Diamond is made up of tightly packed carbon atoms. The Hope diamond is a world-famous deep blue gem that weighs more than 45 carats. You can see this magnificent combination of carbon atoms by visiting the Smithsonian Institution in Washington, D.C.

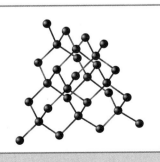

▲ **Figure 2-35** All of these forms of carbon can be mined from the earth. Diamonds come from a mine like this one in South Africa.

Chapter 2 Challenges

Chapter Summary

Lessons 2-1 and 2-2

- Matter is made up of **atoms.** An **element** has only one kind of atom. Elements can be solids, liquids, or gases.
- A **compound** is two or more elements chemically combined. A **molecule** is the smallest part of a compound showing the compound's properties.
- **Chemical symbols** stand for element names. **Chemical formulas** stand for compound names.

Lessons 2-3, 2-4, and 2-5

- **Minerals** are solids formed from elements or compounds. Most rock-forming minerals are made up of compounds. Sand contains the mineral quartz.
- **Physical properties** help identify minerals. Color alone cannot be used to identify a mineral. The color of the powder left by a mineral is called a **streak.**
- Minerals have a metallic or nonmetallic **luster.** The property of a mineral to resist being scratched is called **hardness.**
- **Density** is the amount of matter in a given volume. Every mineral has its own density. Some minerals show **magnetism.** An **acid test** can identify minerals that contain the compound calcium carbonate.

Lessons 2-6 and 2-7

- Minerals are made up of **crystals.** Crystals form in one of six basic crystal systems.
- **Cleavage** is the splitting of minerals into pieces with smooth, flat surfaces. There are different kinds of cleavage. **Fracture** is the splitting of minerals into jagged or uneven pieces.
- **Crystallization** and **evaporation** are some of the processes that form minerals.

Lesson 2-8

- Minerals have many uses. The human body uses minerals. A mineral that contains a useful metal or nonmetal is called an **ore.**
- Gemstones are rare, beautiful, and long-lasting minerals. Cut and polished **gems** are used in jewelry and art.

Key Term Challenges

acid test (p. 50)
atom (p. 42)
chemical formula (p. 44)
chemical symbol (p. 44)
cleavage (p. 52)
compound (p. 42)
crystal (p. 52)
crystallization (p. 54)
density (p. 50)
element (p. 42)
evaporation (p. 54)
fracture (p. 52)
gem (p. 58)
hardness (p. 48)
luster (p. 48)
magnetism (p. 50)
mineral (p. 46)
molecule (p. 42)
ore (p. 58)
physical property (p. 48)
precipitation (p. 54)
solution (p. 54)
streak (p. 48)
subscript (p. 44)

MATCHING Write the Key Term from above that best matches each description.

1. characteristic used to describe objects
2. solid material formed from elements and compounds in Earth's crust
3. the way a mineral reflects light
4. property of a mineral to resist being scratched
5. solid substance with a definite pattern in its atoms
6. amount of mass in a given volume
7. natural force that few minerals show
8. color of a mineral's powder

IDENTIFYING WORD RELATIONSHIPS Explain how the words in each pair are related. Write your answers in complete sentences.

9. gem, ore
10. streak, color
11. cleavage, fracture
12. compound, molecule
13. atom, element
14. chemical symbol, element
15. evaporation, crystallization

Content Challenges TEST PREP

MULTIPLE CHOICE **Write the letter of the term or phrase that best completes each statement.**

1. The smallest part of a compound that has all the properties of that substance is
   a. an atom.
   b. a molecule.
   c. an element.
   d. a formula.

2. CO_2 is
   a. an atom.
   b. a chemical symbol.
   c. a chemical formula.
   d. an element.

3. All materials in Earth's crust are made up of
   a. elements and compounds.
   b. elements and minerals.
   c. silicon and oxygen.
   d. crystals.

4. The softest mineral on Mohs' hardness scale is
   a. quartz.
   b. diamond.
   c. feldspar.
   d. talc.

5. The luster of pyrite can be described as
   a. metallic.
   b. glassy.
   c. dull.
   d. nonmetallic.

6. An acid test is used to test minerals for
   a. quartz.
   b. calcium carbonate.
   c. crystals.
   d. calcium sulfate.

7. The formula for density is
   a. Density = mass ÷ volume.
   b. Density = volume ÷ mass.
   c. Density = volume × mass.
   d. Density = mass × weight.

8. Scientists study the crystal structure of minerals using
   a. a hand lens.
   b. X-rays.
   c. the acid test.
   d. luster.

9. A mineral that breaks into thin, flat sheets is
   a. feldspar.
   b. mica.
   c. asbestos.
   d. quartz.

10. Bodies of water often contain minerals that are
    a. dissolved.
    b. precipitated.
    c. supercooled.
    d. solutions.

TRUE/FALSE **Write *true* if the statement is true. If the statement is false, change the underlined term to make the statement true.**

11. Most elements are <u>liquids</u> at room temperature.

12. A chemical <u>formula</u> stands for one atom of an element.

13. Mohs' scale is used to compare the <u>luster</u> of minerals.

14. There are <u>six</u> basic crystal systems.

15. A mineral with <u>cleavage</u> breaks into pieces with uneven edges.

16. A substance that is not formed from living things or the remains of living things is <u>inorganic</u>.

17. On Mohs' hardness scale, a mineral with a high number <u>cannot</u> scratch a mineral with a lower number.

18. One molecule of <u>CO_2</u> has one atom of carbon and two atoms of oxygen.

Concept Challenges TEST PREP

WRITTEN RESPONSE Answer each of the following questions in complete sentences.

1. **ANALYZE:** Why do you think it is important to test for more than one physical property of a mineral to identify it?
2. **APPLY:** If you were going to buy gold jewelry, what number carat of gold would you choose? Why?
3. **INFER:** Why would the acid test not be useful to identify a diamond?
4. **IDENTIFY:** Glass has a hardness of about 6. What minerals on Mohs' scale will scratch glass?
5. **EXPLAIN:** How would you test an unknown mineral to see if it was magnetite?

INTERPRETING VISUALS Use Figure 2-36 to answer the following questions.

6. Which minerals listed in the table are elements?
7. What element does pyrite have in common with magnetite?
8. Which minerals fracture?
9. Which minerals have a metallic luster?
10. What are the two hardest minerals listed?
11. What property would be most useful in distinguishing between black hematite and magnetite?
12. What are the minerals, in order, from softest to hardest?
13. Why might streak not be a useful property for telling apart quartz and diamond?
14. Which substance can scratch the other—corundum or hematite? Why?
15. Which minerals contain oxygen?
16. How does the chemical formula of magnetite differ from the chemical formula of hematite?

MINERAL PROPERTIES						
Mineral	Chemical Formula	Color	Streak	Luster	Hardness	Fracture or Cleavage
Pyrite	FeS_2	Yellow	Greenish, brownish black	Metallic	6–6.5	Fracture
Magnetite	Fe_3O_4	Black	Black	Metallic	5–6	Fracture
Hematite	Fe_2O_3	Reddish brown to black	Light to dark red	Metallic	5.5–6.5	Fracture
Gold	Au	Gold	Yellow	Metallic	2.5–3	Fracture
Silver	Ag	Silver white	Silver to light gray	Metallic	2.5	Fracture
Diamond	C	Colorless, pale yellow, black	Colorless	Nonmetallic	10	Cleavage
Quartz	SiO_2	Colorless, purple, yellow, pink	Colorless	Nonmetallic	7.5–8	Fracture
Corundum	Al_2O_3	Brown	White	Nonmetallic	9	Fracture

▲ Figure 2-36

Chapter 3 Rocks and Their Origins

▲ **Figure 3-1** The Grand Canyon in northwestern Arizona

The Grand Canyon was cut into rock by the Colorado River. It is more than 1.6 km deep in places and from 6 to 29 km wide. The sides of the canyon are mostly layers of rock. The top has many tall peaks and other interesting landforms. As you can see, much of the canyon is red. However, each rock layer has slightly different coloring—beige and gray; green and pink; brown, silver-gray, and violet.

► The rocks of the Grand Canyon show much about the history of the area. Why do you think the rock layers are different colors?

Contents

3-1 What are rocks?

INVESTIGATE

Observing Rocks
HANDS-ON ACTIVITY

1. Collect some samples of rocks. Draw pictures of them. Describe them in as much detail as you can.
2. Try to scratch all the rocks with a penny. What happens?
3. Use a ruler to measure the rocks and a triple-beam balance to find their mass.
4. Look for different materials within each rock.
5. Look at the rocks through a hand lens. Write down what you see.

THINK ABOUT IT: Do any of the rocks contain mixtures of materials? How do the rocks look different through the hand lens?

STEP 3

Objective
Identify and describe the three classes of rocks.

Key Terms
rock: mixture of minerals, generally cemented together

igneous (IHG-nee-uhs) **rock:** rock formed by the crystallization of hot melted rocks or minerals

sedimentary (sehd-uh-MEHN-tuhr-ee) **rock:** rock formed from pieces of other rocks that are cemented together

metamorphic (meht-uh-MAWR-fihk) **rock:** rock formed when existing rocks are changed by heat and pressure

Rocks in Earth's Crust Earth's crust is made up of many kinds of rocks. **Rocks** are a mixture of minerals usually cemented together.

Small rocks found lying on the ground are fragments of larger rocks. Other rocks are so big that they are part of the landscape, as in Monument Valley in Arizona.

Petrologists (pet-RAH-loh-jists) are Earth science specialists who study rocks and minerals and their origins. They also study rock composition and how rocks change. They can work in deserts, ocean or tropical environments, or arctic areas. They may do studies in areas affected by erosion, earthquakes, or volcanoes.

▲ **Figure 3-2** Monument Valley in northeastern Arizona

All rocks are made up of one or more minerals. There are more than 2,000 different minerals in Earth's crust. However, only a few of these minerals are found in most rocks.

▶ IDENTIFY: What are rocks made up of?

Classification of Rocks The grouping of objects that have certain features in common is called classification. Scientists often classify things to make them easier to study. Biologists classify things as living or nonliving. Chemists classify elements as metals or nonmetals. Petrologists classify rocks and minerals found in Earth's crust. They also classify the types of structures rocks form.

▶ DEFINE: What is classification?

Classes of Rocks Petrologists classify rocks by the way they form. Some rocks form from melted minerals that cool and harden. These rocks are classified as **igneous rocks.** Rocks that form when small pieces of minerals and rocks, or the remains of living things, become cemented or compacted together are classified as **sedimentary rocks.** Other rocks form from existing rocks, which are slowly changed by heat and pressure. These rocks are classified as **metamorphic rocks.**

 IDENTIFY: What are the three classes of rocks?

✓ CHECKING CONCEPTS

1. Rocks are made up of _____.
2. There are more than _____ different minerals in Earth's crust.
3. There are _____ classes of rocks.
4. Rocks are classified as igneous, _____, or metamorphic.
5. When melted minerals cool, _____ rocks form.
6. Scientists who study rocks and minerals are called _____.

THINKING CRITICALLY

7. **INFER:** How would you group rocks to make identifying them easier?
8. **CONTRAST:** How do sedimentary rocks differ from metamorphic rocks?

Web InfoSearch

Stone Monuments A monument is a structure built to honor a person or an event. Many monuments are made of stone, or rock. Different kinds of stone are used for different kinds of monuments. Often, the color, texture, and grain size influence the choice of stone.

SEARCH: Use the Internet to find out about famous stone monuments in the United States. What kinds of stone are they most often made of? Why did the builders choose those kinds of stone? Start your search at www.conceptsandchallenges.com. Some key search words are **national monument, landmarks,** and **statues.**

People in Science
GEOLOGIST

Geologists do many different kinds of work. Some help build roads, dams, and pipelines. Some search for fossil-fuel deposits. Others explore areas for valuable minerals. A petrologist is one type of geologist.

Dr. Michael W. Howell is a marine geologist. He studies deep-sea sediments to learn more about changes in the ocean over time. He analyzes how these changes affected past climates. Dr. Howell also teaches geology at the University of South Carolina. In 2001, he traveled to the Marion Plateau, off the coast of Australia. He was part of an ocean-drilling expedition run by the Ocean Drilling Program.

A geologist can work in industry, for the government, or as a college teacher. To become a geologist, you must complete at least four years of college. Some geologists also pursue postgraduate degrees or degrees from technical institutes.

Thinking Critically Why would a geologist want to drill into the ocean floor?

▲ **Figure 3-3** Here, Dr. Howell is testing deep-sea sediments.

How are igneous rocks formed?

Objective

Identify two ways that igneous rocks are formed.

Key Terms

molten (MOHL-tuhn) **rock:** melted minerals

magma (MAG-muh)**:** molten rock inside Earth

pluton (PLOO-tahn)**:** large body of igneous rock that can form into different shapes when magma cools inside Earth's crust

lava (LAH-vuh)**:** magma that reaches Earth's surface

Heat Inside Earth If you dig about 300 m beneath Earth's surface, the temperature increases about 10°C. As you dig deeper, the temperature gets hotter. The deepest oil wells are drilled about 6 km into Earth's crust. Here, the temperature is more than 60°C. At about 60 km below Earth's surface, in the mantle, it is more than 1,000°C. At about 3,000 km, into the outer core, it is more than 2,200°C. The center of Earth may be as hot as 5,000°C.

Crust
10°C at 300 m

Mantle
1,000°C at 60 km

Outer core
2,200°C at 3,000 km

Inner core
5,000°C at 4,000 km

▲ **Figure 3-4**
Temperatures inside Earth

The temperature of the upper mantle is hot enough to melt minerals and form **molten rock.** When the molten rock cools, it becomes solid, forming igneous rocks.

▲ **Figure 3-6** Basalt is from molten rock that cooled quickly.

1 INFER: Igneous means "formed by fire." Why are rocks formed from magma called igneous?

Magma and Igneous Rocks Molten rock inside Earth is called **magma.** There are large pools of magma inside Earth's upper mantle and lower crust. Sometimes, magma rises through cracks in rocks into the upper part of Earth's crust. Here, the temperature is cooler than the temperature inside the mantle. As magma rises through cracks in Earth's crust, it cools and crystallizes. As it hardens, igneous rock is formed. Igneous rock can take many thousands of years to form from magma.

▼ **Figure 3-5** Large bodies of igneous rock can form above or below ground.

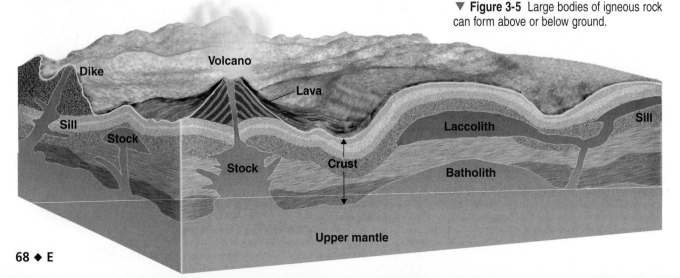

Dike

Volcano

Lava

Sill

Stock

Stock

Crust

Laccolith

Sill

Batholith

Upper mantle

Large bodies of igneous rock with different shapes are formed when magma cools inside Earth's crust. These bodies are called batholiths, stocks, laccoliths, dikes, and sills. A general name for all of these bodies of igneous rock is **pluton.** An example of each kind of pluton is shown in Figure 3-5.

 DEFINE: What is magma?

Lava and Igneous Rocks Sometimes magma rises through cracks in rocks and reaches Earth's surface. Magma that reaches Earth's surface is called **lava.** Lava cools upon contact with air or water. Cooling makes "red hot" lava harden into igneous rock. Igneous rocks form quickly from lava.

 DESCRIBE: How does lava rise to Earth's surface?

☑ CHECKING CONCEPTS

1. Igneous rocks formed from _____ form quickly.
2. Magma that reaches Earth's surface is called _____.

3. Melted minerals form _____ rock.
4. Large pools of _____ are found deep inside Earth.

 THINKING CRITICALLY

5. **PREDICT:** If you were to dig a hole 2 m deep into Earth's surface, would you be likely to find molten rock? Why or why not?
6. **GRAPH:** Make a bar graph comparing the temperatures of the crust, the mantle, the outer core, and the inner core.

Web InfoSearch

Plutons Plutons form inside Earth. However, you can see plutons on Earth's surface in some areas of the United States.

SEARCH: Use the Internet to find out more about plutons. Where can you see them on Earth's surface? How are they exposed? Start your search at www.conceptsandchallenges.com. Some key search words are **plutons, igneous rock,** and **volcano.**

 ## *How Do They Know That?*
THE ORIGIN OF ROCKS

James Hutton (1726–1797) was born in Edinburgh, Scotland. He was trained to be a doctor. However, after Hutton inherited a farm from his father, he became interested in the natural forces at work on Earth's surface. At the time, scientists thought that all rocks were sedimentary rocks. Hutton had a different idea. He said that many rocks, such as granite, were once molten, or melted, rock. Hutton also showed that mountains could be formed by the upward push of igneous rocks. Hutton published his ideas in a book called *Theory of the Earth* in 1795.

Based on his studies of Earth, Hutton proposed a theory about the history of Earth. Hutton's theory said that Earth was shaped in the past by the same forces, such as erosion and sedimentation, that were still at work. Hutton's theory was the beginning of the modern science of geology. Hutton is sometimes called the father of geology.

Thinking Critically Why do you think scientists once thought that all rocks were sedimentary?

▲ **Figure 3-7** James Hutton, the father of geology

Objective

Identify and describe igneous rocks by their minerals and textures.

Key Term

texture (TEHKS-chuhr): size of the crystals in an igneous rock

A Combination of Minerals Igneous rocks are made up of many different kinds of minerals. However, there are only six minerals that are commonly found in igneous rocks. These six common minerals are listed in Figure 3-8.

MINERALS IN IGNEOUS ROCKS		
Quartz	Mica	Amphibole
Feldspar	Olivine	Pyroxene

◀ **Figure 3-8**

Often, igneous rocks can be identified by their minerals. Granite is an igneous rock made up of the minerals known as quartz, feldspar, and mica. Look at the photograph of granite in Figure 3-9. See if you can distinguish the different minerals that make it up.

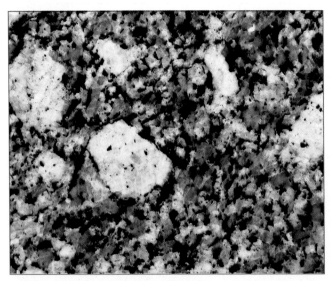

▲ **Figure 3-9** Granite is an igneous rock.

▶ **1** OBSERVE: How do the quartz and feldspar crystals in granite differ?

Crystal Size Igneous rocks have mineral crystals of varying sizes. Crystal size depends on the amount of time it takes the molten rock to cool. The largest crystals form when the rock cools very slowly. Igneous rocks formed from magma have large mineral crystals.

Small crystals take less time to form. Most igneous rocks formed from lava have very small crystals.

Sometimes lava cools so quickly that there is no time for crystals to form. For this reason, a few igneous rocks do not have any crystals. Obsidian is an example of an igneous rock that does not have any crystals.

▲ **Figure 3-10** Obsidian looks like glass because it contains no crystals.

2 INFER: How are cooling rate and crystal size related?

Texture The size of the crystals in an igneous rock is used to describe its **texture**. Texture can be used to identify different igneous rocks that are made up of the same minerals.

For example, you can tell if a rock is granite or rhyolite by looking at its texture. Granite has large crystals that you can see and feel. Rhyolite has very small crystals that are hard to see. Basalt is another commonly found rock with small crystals.

Igneous rocks are classified according to their textures. Igneous rocks with large crystals have a coarse texture. Igneous rocks with small crystals have a fine texture. Igneous rocks that do not have crystals have a glassy texture.

3▶ CLASSIFY: Classify granite, obsidian, basalt, and rhyolite according to their textures.

✓ CHECKING CONCEPTS

1. The six most common minerals in igneous rock are _____, feldspar, mica, olivine, amphibole, and pyroxene.

2. Granite is made up of the minerals quartz, _____, and mica.

3. An igneous rock that has very small mineral crystals most likely was formed from _____.

4. The texture of an igneous rock with no crystals is described as _____.

5. The texture of rhyolite would be described as _____.

💡 THINKING CRITICALLY

6. **ANALYZE:** A rock collector found five igneous rocks. The rocks had mineral crystals with the following sizes: Rock A = 2 mm; Rock B = 7 mm; Rock C = 4.5 mm; Rock D = 10 mm; Rock E = 0.5 mm.

   a. Which rock probably formed from lava?

   b. Which rocks could have formed from magma?

   c. Which rock probably took the longest time to cool?

BUILDING SCIENCE SKILLS

Classifying Scientists often classify igneous rocks according to where they were formed. Igneous rocks that were formed at Earth's surface are called extrusive igneous rocks. Igneous rocks that were formed inside of Earth are called intrusive igneous rocks. Research the roots and prefixes of the terms *intrusive* and *extrusive*. Then, using that information and the information in this lesson, classify granite, obsidian, basalt, and rhyolite as intrusive or extrusive igneous rocks.

Hands-On Activity

CLASSIFYING IGNEOUS ROCKS BY CRYSTAL SIZE

Classifying Igneous Rocks

Rock	Crystal Size	Texture
Diorite		
Gabbro		
Basalt		

▲ **Figure 3-11**

You will need a hand lens; samples of the igneous rocks diorite, gabbro, and basalt; a sheet of paper; and a pencil.

1. Copy the table in Figure 3-11 onto a sheet of paper.

2. Carefully examine each of your rock samples with the hand lens.

3. Record your observations in your table.

Practicing Your Skills

4. **INFER:** Which of these igneous rocks formed deep inside Earth? Explain your answer.

5. **INFER:** Which of these rocks formed on Earth's surface? Explain your answer.

6. **CLASSIFY:** Using information from this lesson, add granite, obsidian, and rhyolite to your table.

▲ **STEP 2** Carefully examine the rock sample with a hand lens.

How are sedimentary rocks formed?

INVESTIGATE

Forming Sedimentary Rock Layers
HANDS-ON ACTIVITY

1. Fill a 12-oz clear plastic jar with water.
2. Measure several spoonfuls each of sand, gravel, clay powder, and fine soil. Put them in the jar.
3. Stir them all together. Observe the color of the mixture.
4. Put a lid on the jar. Let the water sit for a while. Check it again to see the layers that have formed.

THINK ABOUT IT: Do you think the water will remain muddy? Why or why not? How can you tell which materials will end up at the bottom?

◀ **Figure 3-12** Observe the layers that form in your jar.

Objective
Describe two ways that sedimentary rocks are formed.

Key Term
sediment (SEHD-uh-muhnt): rock particles carried and deposited by water, wind, or ice

Sediments What happens when you mix soil and sand in a jar of water? The particles of soil turn to mud and, together with the sand, settle to the bottom of the jar in layers. The sand settles first because it is heavier than the mud. The mud settles on top of the sand. Mud and sand are sediments. **Sediments** are rock particles that are carried and deposited by wind, water, or ice.

 RESTATE: What are sediments?

Natural Cement Many sedimentary rocks form in much the same way as concrete. Concrete is made up of sand, gravel, and cement. Have you ever seen trucks pouring concrete for a building? Inside the trucks, sand, gravel, cement, and water are mixed. A chemical reaction then occurs that causes the sand, gravel, and cement to bind together into concrete. As the water evaporates, the concrete hardens.

How do sedimentary rocks form? Most sedimentary rocks are formed in water. These rocks form from sediments that settle to the bottom of lakes, rivers, or oceans. Over millions of years, the sediments pile up in layers. Some sedimentary rock forms from sediments deposited by wind or glaciers.

The layers of sediment may be hundreds of meters thick. As more sediment is added to the layers, the lower layers of sediment become tightly packed under the pressure and weight of the new layers. The older sediments become solid rock when water and air are squeezed out from between the sediment layers. The sediments may also become solid rock when dissolved minerals in the water cement the sediments together.

▶ DESCRIBE: When does sediment become solid rock?

Sedimentary Rock From Living Things Some types of sedimentary rocks form from the remains of living things. For example, the shells or skeletons of sea animals contain the compound calcium carbonate. When the organisms die, their remains are left on the bottom of the ocean. Over millions of years, the shells and skeletons build up on the ocean floor. Some of the calcium carbonate dissolves and comes out of solution to cement the minerals together. This forms solid rock.

Coquina limestone is a sedimentary rock formed from shells. Chalk limestone also forms from shells. However, you cannot see the shells in it because they were formed from microscopic organisms.

▲ **Figure 3-13** Coquina (left) and chalk (right)

 IDENTIFY: How can shells of marine animals form sedimentary rock?

CHECKING CONCEPTS

1. Why does sand settle to the bottom of a jar faster than mud does?
2. What is sediment?
3. What sedimentary rock is made up of pieces of shells?
4. What are two types of sedimentary rock?

THINKING CRITICALLY

5. **IDENTIFY:** What materials combine together to bind sedimentary rock?
6. **EXPLAIN:** Why does sedimentary rock form in layers?
7. **EXPLAIN:** Why must water evaporate or be pressed out for sedimentary rock to form?
8. **COMPARE/CONTRAST:** How are the rocks chalk and coquina alike and how are they different?
9. **EXPLAIN:** How does weight affect the way in which sediments form layers?

DESIGNING AN EXPERIMENT

Design an experiment to solve the following problem. Include a hypothesis, variables, a procedure, and a type of data to study. Also, tell how to record the data.

PROBLEM: How can you separate salt from sand?

Integrating Life Science

TOPICS: fossils, microorganisms

THE WHITE CLIFFS OF DOVER

The city of Dover is located along the southeastern coast of England. Dover is known for its beautiful white cliffs. These cliffs are composed of deposits of natural chalk and are more than 100 million years old.

How were the White Cliffs of Dover formed? The natural chalk comes from the fossil shells of microscopic animals called foraminifera (for-AM-ih-NIH-fer-ah). Close examination of the chalk deposits reveals the shells of the foraminifera that formed them.

The shells of foraminifera are made up of calcium carbonate ($CaCO_3$). When the foraminifera die, their shells sink to the ocean floor. These shells form fine sediments on the ocean floor. Gradually, the sediments build up until they are hundreds of meters thick. They are then compacted to form solid rock.

▲ **Figure 3-14** The White Cliffs of Dover

▲ **Figure 3-15** Foraminifera

Thinking Critically What compresses the shells of the foraminifera?

How are sedimentary rocks classified?

Objective

Identify and describe the two main groups of sedimentary rocks.

Key Terms

clastic (KLAS-tihk) **rock:** sedimentary rock made up of fragments of rock

nonclastic rock: sedimentary rock made up of dissolved minerals or the remains of living things

Groups of Sedimentary Rocks There are two groups of sedimentary rocks. One group is made up of fragments of rock that have been eroded, transported by water, wind, or ice, and deposited elsewhere. These sedimentary rocks are called **clastic rocks.** Another group of sedimentary rock is made up of dissolved minerals or the remains of plants and animals. These sedimentary rocks are **nonclastic rocks.**

▶ DEFINE: What are clastic rocks?

Particle Size Clastic rocks can be classified according to the sizes and shapes of the sediments that formed them. Conglomerates (kuhn-GLAHM-uhr-aytz) are clastic rocks that are made up of rounded pebbles and gravel.

Sandstones are made of small grains of sand. Shales are clastic rocks made of silt and clay. Silt and clay are the smallest kinds of sediment.

 IDENTIFY: Name three groups of clastic rocks.

▲ **Figure 3-16** Sandstone (top) and shale (bottom)

Dissolved Minerals Most nonclastics form from dissolved minerals. Rocks formed in this way are chemical rocks. When water evaporates from salty lakes and shallow seas, the salts are left behind. These salts form a mineral called halite. Rock salt is a sedimentary rock made up of halite. Some kinds of limestone also form from dissolved minerals. One dissolved mineral that forms limestone is calcite.

Some caves have icicle-shaped deposits of limestone hanging from their ceilings. The cave shown in Figure 3-17 is an example. These deposits are called stalactites (stuh-LAK-tyts). The same cave may also have cone-shaped deposits of limestone rising from its floor. Deposits that rise from the floor are called stalagmites (stuh-LAG-myts).

▼ **Figure 3-17** Icicle-shaped deposits of limestone can be seen in this cave in Lincoln County, New Mexico.

Stalactites and stalagmites are formed from dripping water containing dissolved calcium carbonate. Sometimes, a stalactite and stalagmite may join to form a structure called a column.

 NAME: What mineral makes up rock salt?

Plants and Animals Some nonclastics form from the remains of plants and animals. Rocks formed from the remains of living things are organic rocks. Coals are nonclastic rocks formed from the remains of plants. Coal forms when the remains of plants are compacted for a long time. Coquina and chalk are both nonclastic limestones made up of seashells.

 DESCRIBE: How is coal formed?

✓ CHECKING CONCEPTS

1. Nonclastics are formed from the remains of _____ and _____.
2. Silt and _____ are two kinds of sediment in shale.
3. Caves often have structures called _____ hanging from their ceilings.
4. Coal is a _____ sedimentary rock.

 THINKING CRITICALLY

5. **CLASSIFY:** Which group of nonclastic rock is most likely to form from plants buried for a long time?
6. **CLASSIFY:** Which group of clastic rock might form from the largest kinds of sediment?

Web InfoSearch

Spelunking Exploring caves is called spelunking. People who explore caves are called spelunkers. There are many caves in the United States to explore. If you go spelunking, follow all safety rules. For example, never go spelunking without an experienced spelunker.

SEARCH: Use the Internet to find out more about spelunking. List at least four safety rules you would need to know before entering a cave. Also, list the equipment you would need. Start your search at www.conceptsandchallenges.com. Some key search words are **spelunking, cave exploring,** and **stalactite.**

 Hands-On Activity

FORMING CLASTIC ROCK

You will need safety goggles, three plastic foam cups, a tablespoon (tbsp), plaster of Paris, sand, pebbles, and water.

1. In one cup, stir together 2 tbsp each of sand and plaster of Paris. Add 1 tbsp of water. Stir.
2. In the second cup, stir together 1 tbsp each of pebbles, sand, and water. Add 2 tbsp of plaster of Paris and stir. Spoon this mixture on top of the mixture in the first cup.
3. In the third cup, prepare the same mixture as in Step 1. Spoon it on top of the other two layers in the first cup. Set the cup aside to harden.
4. The next day, peel away the cup from the clastic rock you created. Scrape away the surface from the side of the rock.

▲ **STEP 3** Spoon the mixture on top of the other layers.

Practicing Your Skills

5. **DESCRIBE:** What does the side of your rock look like?
6. **OBSERVE:** What kinds of particles does each layer have?

3-6 How are metamorphic rocks formed?

Objective
Describe two ways in which metamorphic rocks form.

Changed Rocks You can make bread from water, flour, salt, and yeast. First, you mix the ingredients. Then, you bake the mixture in an oven. After baking the mixture, you will not recognize any of the ingredients. The heat of the oven changes the water, flour, salt, and yeast.

The inside of Earth is like an oven. Heat and pressure inside Earth "bakes" rocks and changes the minerals in them. These chemically changed rocks are called metamorphic rocks.

▶ 1 EXPLAIN: Why are metamorphic rocks called changed rocks?

Heat and Pressure Minerals in all types of rocks go through chemical changes when the rocks are heated. Minerals go through chemical changes at temperatures of between 200°C and 800°C. Minerals do not change chemically when the temperature is below 100°C. Above 800°C, the minerals melt into magma, or molten rock.

Rocks buried deep inside Earth's crust are also affected by forces. These forces cause pressure, which changes the form of minerals. Extreme pressure can flatten minerals into layers, as shown in Figure 3-18.

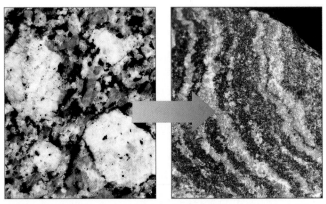

▲ **Figure 3-19** Pressure may cause minerals in rock to form into bands in metamorphic rock. Here granite (left), an igneous rock, becomes gneiss (right), a metamorphic rock.

▶ 2 EXPLAIN: What can flatten minerals into layers?

Magma Metamorphic rocks are sometimes formed when existing rocks come into contact with or mix with magma. Magma can move into cracks in deeply buried sedimentary rocks. It may also flow between the layers of sedimentary rocks. The heat and chemical solutions in the magma cause the minerals inside the sedimentary rocks to change. The heat from magma can also change minerals in igneous rocks and turn one kind of metamorphic rock into a different kind of metamorphic rock.

▶ 3 IDENTIFY: What kinds of rocks are changed by coming into contact with magma?

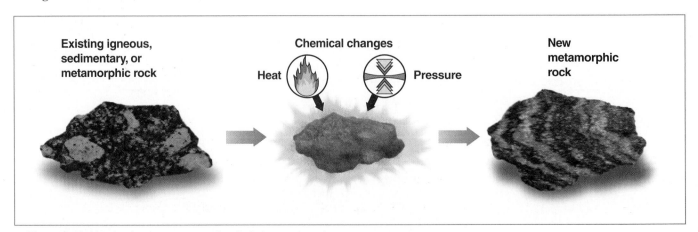

Existing igneous, sedimentary, or metamorphic rock → Chemical changes — Heat — Pressure → New metamorphic rock

▲ **Figure 3-18** Heat and pressure cause chemical changes in rock.

1. Igneous and sedimentary rocks can be changed into metamorphic rocks by _____ and _____.

2. Minerals in deeply buried rocks are flattened by great _____.

3. The minerals in rocks can be changed by the heat and chemical solutions in _____.

4. Pressure is caused by _____ that push against an object.

5. When rocks are heated to 200°C, the minerals in the rocks go through a _____ change.

THINKING CRITICALLY

6. **DESCRIBE:** What happens to the minerals in rocks that are heated to a temperature of less than 100°C?

7. **DESCRIBE:** What happens to the minerals in rocks that are heated to a temperature of 950°C?

8. **PREDICT:** Would the minerals in a rock buried 2 m beneath Earth's surface be significantly affected by pressure? Explain.

Web InfoSearch

Stonemasonry In stonemasonry, stonemasons build structures using many types of stone from all around the world. Some of the most popular building stones are granite, marble, and slate. Stonemasons measure, cut, and carve stone to a specific shape or form. The stones are used in new and restored buildings. For restored buildings, the masons must often keep the new stonework as close as possible to the original stonework.

SEARCH: Use the Internet to find out more about stonemasonry. Are there different types of stonemasons? What training do you need to perform the job? What skills and interests should you have? After finishing your research, write a help wanted ad for a stonemason to restore old stone fireplaces. Start your search at www.conceptsandchallenges.com. Some key search words are **stonemasonry, fireplace restoration,** and **masonry.**

Integrating Physical Science

TOPICS: force, pressure

CALCULATING PRESSURE

The definition of pressure is force per unit of area. Pressure changes rocks and affects the atmosphere and oceans. The amount of pressure applied to an object can be calculated using the following formula:

$$\text{Pressure} = \text{force} \div \text{area}$$

In this formula, force is measured in units called newtons (N). A 1 kg weight exerts a downward force of 9.8 N. Area is measured in square units.

You can calculate pressure using the formula above. Suppose a person exerts a force of 120 N while pressing down on something with the heel of his or her shoe. The heel of the shoe has an area of 60 cm². What would the pressure be? Of course, in the real world, the entire weight of a person may not be concentrated on his or her heel.

Thinking Critically When would you not put all your weight into stepping down?

▲ **Figure 3-20** Footprints in sand show the force of pressure.

3-7 How are metamorphic rocks classified?

Objective
Explain the difference between foliated and nonfoliated metamorphic rocks.

Key Terms
foliated (FOH-lee-ay-tuhd): texture of a metamorphic rock that has mineral crystals arranged in bands

nonfoliated: texture of a metamorphic rock that does not have mineral crystals arranged in bands

Classifying Metamorphic Rocks Petrologists classify metamorphic rocks based on the texture of the rock. Metamorphic rocks have two kinds of textures, foliated and nonfoliated. The texture of a metamorphic rock is determined by the arrangement of its mineral crystals.

CLASSIFICATION OF METAMORPHIC ROCKS		
Original Rock	**Metamorphic Rock**	**Texture**
Granite, shale	Gneiss	Foliated
Granite, shale, basalt	Schist	Foliated
Shale	Slate	Foliated
Sandstone	Quartzite	Nonfoliated
Limestone	Marble	Nonfoliated

▲ Figure 3-21

1 CLASSIFY: How are metamorphic rocks grouped?

Banded Metamorphic Rocks The mineral crystals in some metamorphic rocks are arranged in bands. The texture of a metamorphic rock with minerals arranged in bands is called **foliated.** Foliated rocks tend to break along their mineral crystal bands.

Foliated metamorphic rocks are formed when existing rocks are placed under great heat and pressure. Under this great heat and pressure, the minerals in the rocks melt and recrystallize into minerals that form bands.

Gneiss (NICE) is a foliated metamorphic rock. Gneiss is formed when granite is put under great heat and pressure.

Schist is another rock that has bands of recrystallized minerals. Schist is formed from shale, basalt, or granite. Slate is also formed from shale.

▲ Figure 3-22 Shale (left) becomes slate (right).

2 COMPARE: How are gneiss and schist similar?

Metamorphic Rocks Without Bands The texture of a metamorphic rock that does not have its minerals arranged in bands is **nonfoliated.** Nonfoliated metamorphic rocks do not break in layers.

Marble and quartzite are nonfoliated metamorphic rocks. Marble is formed from limestone. Marble contains large mineral crystals of calcite.

Quartzite is formed from sandstone put under great heat and pressure. Quartzite has large crystals of quartz.

▲ Figure 3-23 Limestone (left) becomes marble (right).

3 IDENTIFY: Which metamorphic rock has large crystals of quartz formed from sand?

✔ CHECKING CONCEPTS

1. What are the two textures of metamorphic rock?
2. What causes banding in metamorphic rock?
3. How do foliated rocks break?
4. A metamorphic rock without banding has what kind of texture?

💡 THINKING CRITICALLY

Use Figure 3-21 to answer the following questions.

5. INTERPRET: Which metamorphic rocks are formed when granite is subjected to high heat and pressure?
6. INTERPRET: Which metamorphic rock is formed from limestone?
7. INTERPRET: Which metamorphic rocks can be formed from shale?
8. INTERPRET: From which sedimentary rock is quartzite formed?
9. CLASSIFY: Is slate a foliated or a nonfoliated metamorphic rock? Why?

BUILDING SCIENCE SKILLS

Researching Metamorphic rocks, such as marble and slate, are economically important. Use the Internet or reference books to find out where in the United States deposits of marble and slate can be found. Determine how these varieties of rock are different from those found elsewhere, such as in Italy. Also, find out how the impurities in the rocks give them their special colors. Finally, list some ways in which marble and slate are important to business and industry.

▲ **Figure 3-24** India's Taj Mahal is made of white marble from India.

 Real-Life Science

MARBLE IN ART AND ARCHITECTURE

▲ **Figure 3-25** The Lincoln Memorial in Washington, D.C.

Marble is often used in architecture and sculpture because it is beautiful to look at and lasts a long time. The Lincoln Memorial was built to honor our sixteenth president, Abraham Lincoln. Construction began in 1914. It was not completed until 1922.

The Piccirilli brothers, both well-known marble sculptors, were chosen to carve the statue. It is 5.8 m tall and contains 28 blocks of white Georgia marble. The statue itself took four years to complete. The outside of the memorial contains marble from Colorado and Tennessee. The ceiling looks clear. The marble used in it was soaked in a waxy, whitish mixture known as paraffin to make it shine.

Another famous memorial made of marble is the Taj Mahal in India. It was built by an emperor in the 1600s to honor his wife.

Are there buildings or statues in your town that contain marble? Take a walk around your community and see if you can find some.

Thinking Critically What kind of rock is marble?

3-8 What is the rock cycle?

Objective
Explain the rock cycle.

Key Terms

cycle: series of events that happen over and over again

rock cycle: series of natural processes by which rocks are slowly changed from one kind of rock to another kind of rock

Nature's Cycles A series of events that happen over and over again for a certain length of time is called a **cycle.** In nature, there are many different cycles. If you look around you, you will probably find many different examples of nature's cycles.

The rise and fall of the ocean tides is a natural cycle that occurs twice each day. The movement of Earth around the Sun is a natural cycle that takes a year to complete. The Moon going through its phases is another cycle.

1 ▶ DEFINE: What is a cycle?

The Rock Cycle Rocks on Earth change over time. Some of the changes in rocks take place inside Earth. There, tremendous heat and pressure can slowly change rocks from one kind of rock into another. Other changes in rocks take place at the surface. On Earth's surface, rocks may be changed by rain, ice, wind, or the action of chemicals in air or water. The series of natural processes by which rocks are slowly changed from one kind of rock to another kind of rock is called the **rock cycle.** Look at the diagram of the rock cycle in Figure 3-26. It shows the ways that rocks are changed from one rock type to another.

2 ▶ INFER: How do you think ice, rain, and wind can change rocks?

A Closer Look at the Rock Cycle Look again at the diagram of the rock cycle. Notice that all three classes of rock eventually lead to sedimentary rock. The three classes of rocks can also be changed into metamorphic rocks or back into magma. However, only igneous rocks form directly from magma.

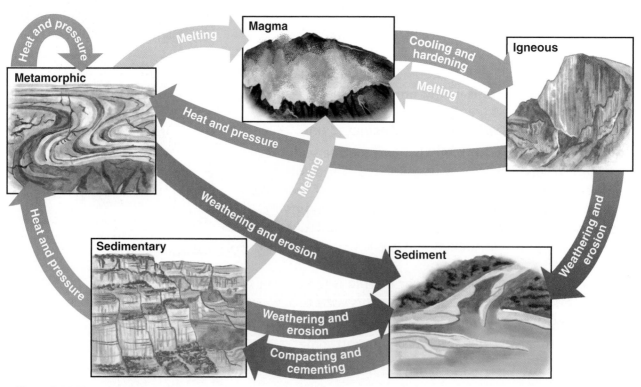

▲ **Figure 3-26** The rock cycle

At Earth's surface, rocks are broken apart by the forces of nature—moving water, ice, plant action, and wind. The particles of rock may then settle in lakes or oceans to form sediment that eventually makes up sedimentary rock.

Deeply buried igneous and sedimentary rocks can change into metamorphic rock or melt back into magma. Intense heat and pressure can change any rock into metamorphic rock. High temperatures can change any rock back into magma.

 OBSERVE: How does magma become igneous rock?

✓ CHECKING CONCEPTS

1. What changes rock inside Earth?
2. What can all rocks be broken down into?
3. What kind of rock does magma cool and harden into?
4. What two conditions slowly change one type of rock into another?

THINKING CRITICALLY

5. **COMPARE:** How is the rock cycle like other natural cycles on Earth?
6. **INFER:** Why can only igneous rocks be formed directly from magma?
7. **APPLY:** Look around your neighborhood. What examples can you find of the rock cycle in action? What do you think caused the rocks to change?

INTERPRETING VISUALS

Use Figure 3-26 to answer the following questions.

8. **EXPLAIN:** How can igneous or metamorphic rock eventually become sedimentary rock?
9. **IDENTIFY:** What processes change sedimentary rock into metamorphic rock?
10. **NAME:** What processes or forces change metamorphic rock into igneous rock?

Hands-On Activity

CLASSIFYING ROCKS BY TYPE

You will need 10 different rocks, a hand lens, stickers, paper, pencil, and (optional) a field guide to rocks or other reference books.

1. Collect 10 different rocks from around your town. Label each rock with a numbered sticker.
2. Look at each rock with a hand lens. Record your observations on a sheet of paper.
3. Using your notes, classify each rock as sedimentary, igneous, or metamorphic.
4. Using reference materials, identify as many of your rock samples as you can. Write the name of each rock in your notes.

▲ **STEP 2** Use a hand lens to study each rock.

Practicing Your Skills

5. **CLASSIFY:** How many rocks did you classify as igneous? How many rocks did you classify as sedimentary? How many rocks did you classify as metamorphic? Explain your choices.
6. **EXPLAIN:** How many rocks were you not able to identify? Why weren't you able to identify these?

LAB ACTIVITY
Modeling What Lies Beneath Earth's Surface

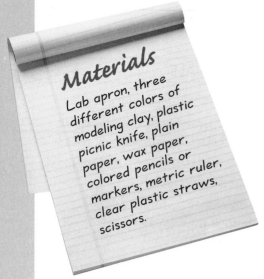

Materials
Lab apron, three different colors of modeling clay, plastic picnic knife, plain paper, wax paper, colored pencils or markers, metric ruler, clear plastic straws, scissors.

BACKGROUND

Beneath Earth's surface lies a complex structure of rock layers. These layers provide clues as to how Earth's crust formed. Geologists drill deep into these layers of rock. The drills are like apple corers. They bring up rock cores for study.

PURPOSE

In this activity, you will work with a group to create a model of a hill made up of several rock layers. You will then trade your model for the model created by another group. Using clear plastic straws, you will determine what lies beneath the surface and make a profile graph.

PROCEDURE

1. Put on your lab apron.

2. Each color of clay should represent a different type of rock. For example, yellow could be sedimentary rock; blue, metamorphic rock; and red, igneous rock. Place a lump of modeling clay on a sheet of wax paper. Shape the clay to form a gentle hill.

3. Add additional layers to the hill using colored clay. Create a gentle hill 4 cm high and 20 cm wide. The top layer should cover all the layers below.

4. Exchange your model with one made by another group.

5. Use the ruler and a pencil to make a light line straight across the model at its widest point (20 cm). This is your profile line.

▲ **STEP 3** Add layers to your hill using different colors of clay.

▲ **STEP 5** Make a line straight across your model.

6. Draw a straight line 20 cm long on a sheet of paper.

7. Place the end of a straw along the profile line on one end of the hill. Twirl the straw and slowly push it through the clay to the tabletop. Remove the straw. It will have a core sample inside. Cut the straw a short distance above the clay core sample.
⚠ CAUTION: Be careful when using scissors.

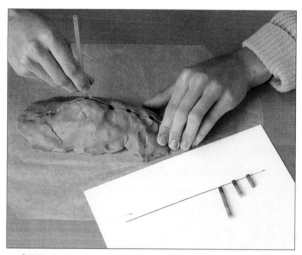
▲ STEP 7 Slowly push the straw through the clay to the tabletop.

8. Place the lower edge of the core sample on the 20-cm line that you drew. The core should be in the same place on the line as it was on the model.

9. Using the remainder of the straw, take other core samples a few centimeters apart along the profile line until you have sampled the length of the hill.

10. Use colored pencils or markers to fill in the spaces on the paper between your core samples. This will complete the profile diagram.

11. Slice the clay model in half along the profile line. Compare the clay model to the profile diagram.

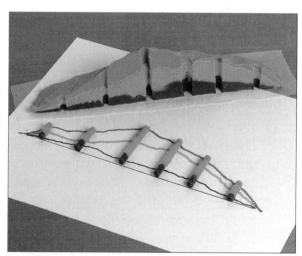
▲ STEP 11 Compare your model to the diagram you made.

CONCLUSIONS

1. OBSERVE: How close was the profile graph you drew to the model?

2. OBSERVE: How many core samples did you take? Could you have used fewer cores?

3. INFER: How do profile graphs help geologists determine the history of a region on Earth?

Integrating Physical Science

THE Big IDEA

What drives the rock cycle?

The rocks in Earth's crust are constantly being changed. These changes are caused by forces pushing and pulling rocks in all directions.

Have you ever been in a tug-of-war contest? If so, then you know that you pull on a rope together with other members of your team. Your team exerts a force on the rope. If that force is greater than the force exerted by the other team, the rope is pulled toward you, and your team wins the contest!

Forces are exerted on Earth's rocks, too. The effects of these push-pull forces create pressure. This pressure causes bits and pieces of rocks and minerals to join together into sedimentary rock. Metamorphic rocks form from pressure deep beneath Earth's surface.

Gravity is also a force at work in the rock cycle. Gravity causes sediments in water to sink to the bottom. Also, gravity causes the weight of rock layers on top to press down on rock layers below. This, in turn, causes compaction.

Heat is a form of energy. Heat can change rock. When the minerals in rocks are under great heat and pressure, they may melt and combine chemically to form metamorphic rock.

Removing heat from a substance also causes changes in rocks. When a substance cools, it loses heat energy. Its molecules slow down and move closer together. The substance hardens to form a solid. Igneous rocks form this way. As the molten rock moves towards Earth's surface, it cools. Molecules in the molten rock slow down, and minerals crystallize to form igneous rock.

Look at the illustrations on these two pages. Then, follow the instructions in the Science Log to learn more about "the big idea." ◆

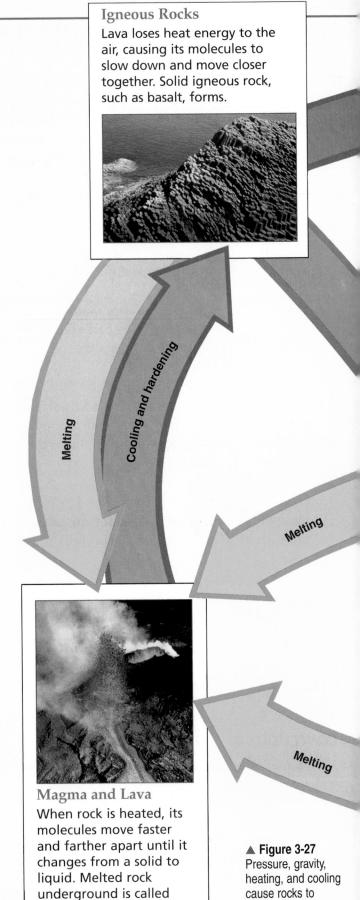

Igneous Rocks
Lava loses heat energy to the air, causing its molecules to slow down and move closer together. Solid igneous rock, such as basalt, forms.

Melting

Cooling and hardening

Melting

Melting

Magma and Lava
When rock is heated, its molecules move faster and farther apart until it changes from a solid to liquid. Melted rock underground is called magma. Above ground it is called lava.

▲ **Figure 3-27**
Pressure, gravity, heating, and cooling cause rocks to continually change form throughout the rock cycle.

84 ◆ E

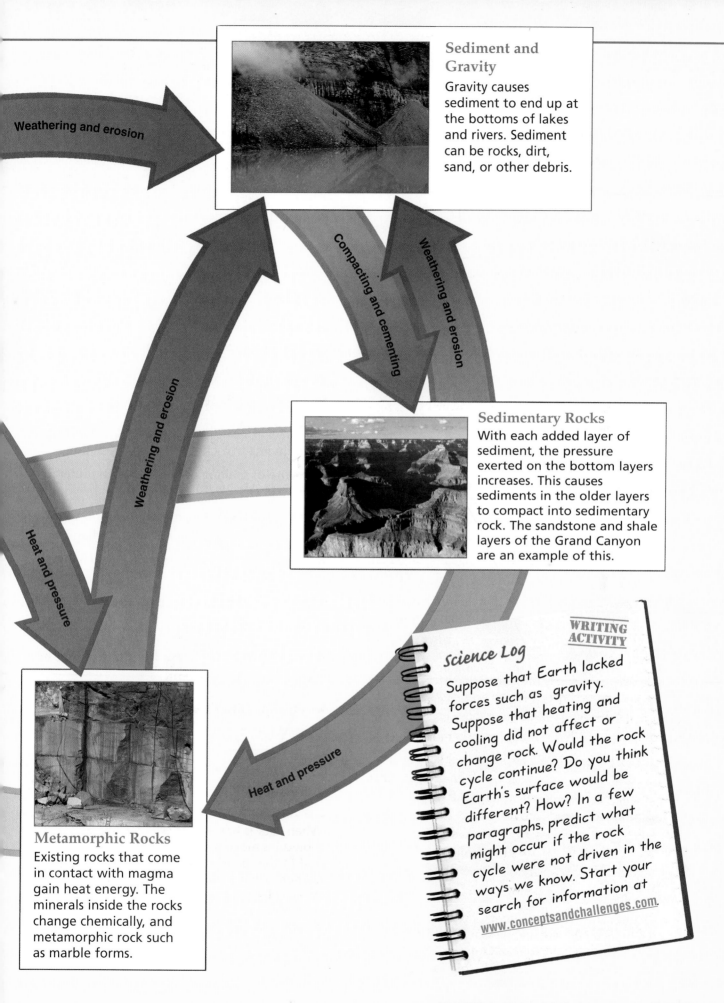

Sediment and Gravity

Gravity causes sediment to end up at the bottoms of lakes and rivers. Sediment can be rocks, dirt, sand, or other debris.

Weathering and erosion

Compacting and cementing

Weathering and erosion

Weathering and erosion

Heat and pressure

Sedimentary Rocks

With each added layer of sediment, the pressure exerted on the bottom layers increases. This causes sediments in the older layers to compact into sedimentary rock. The sandstone and shale layers of the Grand Canyon are an example of this.

Heat and pressure

Metamorphic Rocks

Existing rocks that come in contact with magma gain heat energy. The minerals inside the rocks change chemically, and metamorphic rock such as marble forms.

WRITING ACTIVITY

Science Log

Suppose that Earth lacked forces such as gravity. Suppose that heating and cooling did not affect or change rock. Would the rock cycle continue? Do you think Earth's surface would be different? How? In a few paragraphs, predict what might occur if the rock cycle were not driven in the ways we know. Start your search for information at www.conceptsandchallenges.com.

Chapter Summary

Lesson 3-1

- **Rocks** are made up of one or more minerals. The three types of rock are **igneous, sedimentary,** and **metamorphic.**

Lessons 3-2 and 3-3

- **Igneous rocks** form from **magma.** Magma is **molten rock** inside Earth.
- **Lava** is magma that has reached Earth's surface.
- The minerals in an igneous rock can be used to identify the rock.
- Crystal size is influenced by the rate at which molten rock cools. Crystal size in igneous rock determines its **texture.** Igneous rocks can be classified according to their textures.

Lessons 3-4 and 3-5

- **Sediment** is small pieces of rocks and minerals and the remains of living things that settle to the bottom of water. **Sedimentary rock** is formed when sediments are cemented together by dissolved minerals.
- **Clastics** and **nonclastics** are two groups of sedimentary rock. Clastics are classified according to the size and shape of their sediments. Nonclastics form from minerals dissolved in water or from the remains of plants and animals.

Lessons 3-6 and 3-7

- **Metamorphic rock** is formed when great heat and pressure inside Earth chemically change the minerals in rocks. The heat and chemical solutions in magma can also change the minerals in rocks.
- Metamorphic rocks have two kinds of textures. The mineral crystals in **foliated** metamorphic rocks are arranged in bands. The texture of a metamorphic rock that does not have bands is called **nonfoliated.**

Lesson 3-8

- The **rock cycle** is a series of natural processes by which rocks slowly change from one kind of rock to another kind of rock.
- All rocks can change into another type of rock or back to magma. Heat and pressure can change any rock into metamorphic rock.

Key Term Challenges

clastic rock (p. 74)
cycle (p. 80)
foliated (p. 78)
igneous rock (p. 66)
lava (p. 68)
magma (p. 68)
metamorphic rock (p. 66)
molten rock (p. 68)
nonclastic rock (p. 74)
nonfoliated (p. 78)
pluton (p. 68)
rock (p. 66)
rock cycle (p. 80)
sediment (p. 72)
sedimentary rock (p. 66)
texture (p. 70)

MATCHING **Write the Key Term from above that best matches each description.**

1. rock formed from molten material
2. magma that reaches Earth's surface
3. size of crystals in a rock
4. sedimentary rocks from dissolved minerals
5. texture of metamorphic rock with mineral crystals arranged in bands
6. texture of metamorphic rock that does not have mineral crystals arranged in bands
7. rock formed when another rock is changed by heat and pressure
8. process that occurs over and over

FILL IN **Write the Key Term from above that best completes each statement.**

9. A rock that forms when rocks and minerals are cemented together is classified as a _____.
10. Conglomerates belong to a group of sedimentary rocks called _____.
11. Molten rock inside Earth is called _____.
12. The process by which rocks slowly change from one kind of rock to another is the _____.
13. Rock materials that settle in water are called _____.
14. A large body of igneous rock formed by magma cooling is called a _____.

Content Challenges TEST PREP

MULTIPLE CHOICE Write the letter of the term or phrase that best completes each statement.

1. All rocks are made up of one or more
   a. sediments.
   b. minerals.
   c. magmas.
   d. metals.

2. A scientist who studies and classifies rocks is a
   a. chemist.
   b. geographer.
   c. biologist.
   d. petrologist.

3. The kind of rock formed when melted minerals cool and harden is
   a. molten rock.
   b. sedimentary rock.
   c. igneous rock.
   d. metamorphic rock.

4. A rock formed when an existing rock is changed by heat and pressure is
   a. molten rock.
   b. sedimentary rock.
   c. igneous rock.
   d. metamorphic rock.

5. Rocks formed from once-living things are usually classified as
   a. molten rocks.
   b. igneous rocks.
   c. sedimentary rocks.
   d. metamorphic rocks.

6. Magma that reaches Earth's surface cools and hardens into
   a. igneous rock.
   b. sedimentary rock.
   c. molten rock.
   d. metamorphic rock.

7. The only kind of rock that can form directly from magma is
   a. sedimentary rock.
   b. molten rock.
   c. igneous rock.
   d. metamorphic rock.

8. Crystal size in an igneous rock is determined by the rate at which the magma in the rock
   a. cools.
   b. melts.
   c. reaches Earth's surface.
   d. freezes.

9. Silt and sand are examples of
   a. molten rock.
   b. magma.
   c. lava.
   d. sediments.

TRUE/FALSE Write *true* if the statement is true. If the statement is false, change the underlined term to make the statement true.

10. Most nonclastic sedimentary rocks are made up of <u>mud</u>.

11. Magma that reaches Earth's surface is called <u>lava</u>.

12. <u>Metamorphic</u> rocks are formed when existing rocks are changed by heat and pressure.

13. The texture of a <u>sedimentary</u> rock that does not have minerals arranged in bands is described as nonfoliated.

14. Limestone is formed from dissolved <u>halite</u>.

15. <u>Igneous</u> rocks can be identified by their minerals.

16. Igneous rocks formed from lava usually have <u>large</u> crystals.

17. Marble is an <u>igneous</u> rock formed when limestone is heated.

18. Slate is a <u>foliated</u> metamorphic rock.

Concept Challenges TEST PREP

WRITTEN RESPONSE Answer each of the following questions in complete sentences.

1. EXPLAIN: The law of conservation of matter states that matter cannot be created or destroyed. However, matter can be changed from one form to another. Explain how the rock cycle supports the law of conservation of matter.

2. CLASSIFY: Pumice is a kind of rock often formed from volcanic lava. In what class of rocks should pumice be classified?

3. EXPLAIN: What is the difference between magma and lava?

4. CONTRAST: How do igneous rocks formed from lava differ from igneous rocks formed from magma?

5. CLASSIFY: Slate is a metamorphic rock that breaks into sheets along its crystal bands. Is slate foliated or nonfoliated metamorphic rock? Explain your answer.

INTERPRETING VISUALS Use Figure 3-28 below to answer the following questions.

6. What are the three types of rock?

7. How does magma form igneous rock?

8. What processes break down igneous rocks into sediments?

9. What happens when the minerals in igneous, sedimentary, and metamorphic rocks melt?

10. How do igneous rocks change into metamorphic rocks?

11. What are two kinds of rock that can form sedimentary rock?

12. What is the only kind of rock that can form directly from magma?

13. What kinds of rocks can form metamorphic rocks?

14. When does the rock cycle end? Explain.

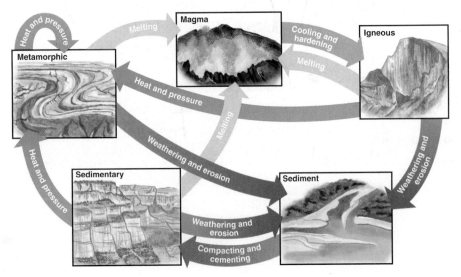

◀ **Figure 3-28** The rock cycle

Chapter 4 The Rock Record

▲ **Figure 4-1** A plant fossil imprint in sedimentary rock

Fossils are important tools for reconstructing the distant, or geologic, past. They give us clues as to what life was like on Earth millions of years ago, when the environment was different. Knowing the different species that existed at different times can help us guess what the climate and land were like at those times. Fossils can also help scientists match rocks of similar ages from different locations.

▶How might the land during earlier ages have been different from today?

Contents

4-1 How are organisms preserved?

INVESTIGATE

Making a Time Capsule
HANDS-ON ACTIVITY

1. A time capsule is one way to preserve objects and information for people of the future. To make your own time capsule, get a very large plastic container with a lid.

2. Put an object in the container. Have five of your classmates each place an object in it.

3. Write something down about each of the objects in the container. Put the note inside.

4. Close the lid.

5. Find an appropriate place to bury the container in the ground.

THINK ABOUT IT: Why did you include the objects you did in your time capsule? Why did you bury the time capsule where you did?

Objectives
Define fossils. Describe how organisms are preserved in rock and elsewhere.

Key Terms
fossil (FAHS-uhl)**:** remains or traces of an organism that lived long ago

mold: imprint or hollow in rock that is shaped like and made by an organism

cast: mold filled with hardened sediments

amber: hardened tree sap

What Are Fossils?   The remains or traces of organisms that lived long ago are called **fossils.** A fossil can be a bone, a whole skeleton, an imprint, a shell, or even the body of an ancient species.

▲ **Figure 4-2** *Tyrannosaurus rex* was a very large, carnivorous dinosaur that lived more than 65 million years ago.

Many species that lived long ago are extinct. That means they are no longer found alive on Earth. Dinosaurs are extinct. However, their remains have been found in many places.

1 DEFINE: What are fossils?

Fossils in Rock   Most fossils are found in sedimentary rock that was once under water. It takes millions of years for fossils to form. A fossil begins to form when an organism dies and is buried quickly by sediment. The soft parts of the organism decay. Usually, only the hard parts, such as shells and bones, are left. Through chemical processes, the sediments slowly harden into rock.

Sometimes, as the organism decays, it leaves a hollow opening in a rock. This hollow opening is called a **mold.** Later, the mold may fill up with sand or mud that later hardens. This material forms a **cast.**

Some fossils are only imprints, or marks, of the organisms in the rock. For example, footprints are made when an animal steps into soft mud. The mud hardens

▲ **Figure 4-3** Some fish imprints show the bones of the fish.

into rock, preserving the footprint. Scientists have also found many fish and leaf imprints.

2 NAME: What kind of rock contains the most fossils?

Fossils in Ice and Tar Freezing helps preserve things by preventing decay. The bodies of about 50 elephant-like extinct animals called mammoths have been found frozen in Siberian and Alaskan soil and ice. Wooly rhinoceroses have also been found.

▲ Figure 4-4 Museum model of a wooly mammoth

Animal remains have also been found in ancient pits of thick, sticky tar. These tar pits often become covered by water. Animals that went to them to drink were trapped in the tar. Other animals that tried to eat the trapped animals also became trapped. The animals sank into the tar and were preserved. In southern California, the bones of extinct animals such as saber-toothed cats and dire wolves have been found in the LaBrea tar pits. Parts of extinct camels, mastodons, vultures, and bison have also been found there. Tarlike oil deposits in Poland contained entire specimens of wooly rhinoceroses.

▲ Figure 4-5 The skeleton of a saber-toothed cat

3 IDENTIFY: How are animals trapped in tar pits?

Fossils in Amber
A clear, sticky sap flows from some kinds of trees. This hardened tree sap is called **amber.** Millions of years ago, many insects and leaf fragments became trapped in the sticky sap. More sap covered these organisms. The sap hardened, and the organisms were perfectly preserved inside.

▲ Figure 4-6 Insects are often found perfectly preserved in amber.

4 DEFINE: What is amber made from?

☑ CHECKING CONCEPTS

1. What four substances help preserve the remains of organisms?
2. What animal parts are most often preserved?
3. Which extinct animals were preserved in ice?
4. What else besides plants are usually preserved in amber?

💡 THINKING CRITICALLY

5. INFER: How do we know that dinosaurs existed?
6. HYPOTHESIZE: Why are fossils rarely found in igneous rocks?
7. PREDICT: Which of the following would most likely be found as a fossil: a clam shell, a flower petal, or an ancient worm? Why?

Web InfoSearch

Petrified Fossils Sometimes fossils are preserved by a process called petrification. To *petrify* means to "turn to stone."

SEARCH: Use the Internet to find out more about petrification. How does the process work, and exactly what does it do to the organism? Start your search at www.conceptsandchallenges.com. Some key search words are **fossils, petrified forest,** and **petrification.**

LAB ACTIVITY
Modeling a Fossil Formation

Materials
Safety goggles, lab apron, modeling clay, sugar cubes, small jar or disposable plastic food tub, wax paper (15-cm square), small seashells or snail shells, plaster of Paris, water, mixing tub, large spoon, toothpicks

BACKGROUND

Many sedimentary rocks contain the remains of ancient animal and plant life. These remains are called fossils. A seashell, bone, or leaf is buried in sediment. Its remains may leave an impression in the sediment. Fossil impressions are called molds. Later, more sediment fills in the mold and hardens. These fossils are called casts.

PURPOSE

In this activity, you will experiment with creating fossil molds and casts.

PROCEDURE

1. Put on your lab apron.

2. Place the square of wax paper on your table and spread a small lump of clay on it. Press a sugar cube into the clay.

3. Remove the clay with sugar cube from the wax paper and place them in a container with cold water. Set it aside and leave it overnight.

4. Place a larger lump of clay on the wax paper. Flatten it out. Pinch up the edges to form a shallow dish.

5. Press a small seashell or snail shell into the clay to make an impression. Gently remove the shell. You can make more impressions with different shells if there is extra clay.

▲ **STEP 2** Press a sugar cube into the clay.

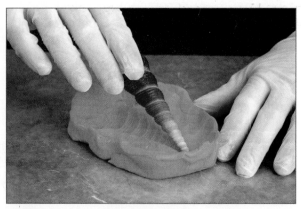

▲ **STEP 5** Make an impression with your seashell.

6. Mix the plaster of Paris with just enough water to make it easy to pour.

7. Gently spoon plaster into your dish to fill it. You must leave the plaster to set overnight. Place a small nametag next to your clay dish to identify it.

8. After a full day has passed, examine your sugar cube experiment and answer the questions below. Then, gently remove the clay from the outside of your plaster fossil. If any bits stick to the model, you can clean them off with toothpicks. Compare your fossil to the shell that made it. Copy the chart in Figure 4-7 and record your observations.

▲ **STEP 7** Spoon enough plaster of Paris into the clay dish to fill it.

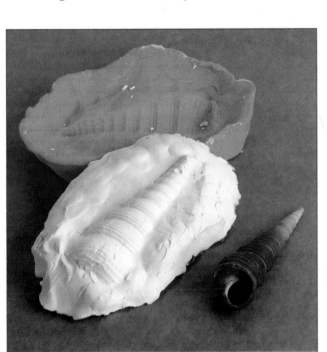

▲ **STEP 8** Compare your plaster fossil shell with the shell from which it was made.

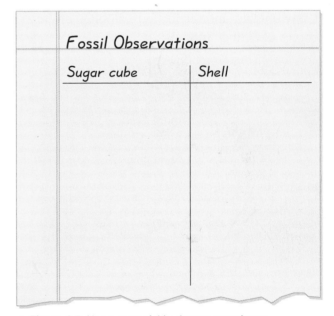

▲ **Figure 4-7** Use a copy of this chart to record your observations.

Fossil Observations

Sugar cube	Shell

CONCLUSIONS

1. **OBSERVE:** What happened to the sugar cube?

2. **ANALYZE:** Why did the change take place?

3. **APPLY:** How are fossils of life forms made in rocks?

4. **IDENTIFY:** What two kinds of fossils did you make?

4-2 Why do scientists study fossils?

Objective
Explain how fossils are clues to Earth's history.

Key Terms
coprolite (KAHP-roh-lyt): fossil dung or the stomach contents of ancient animals

gastrolith (GAS-troh-lihth): stone used to grind food

The History of Life on Earth Fossils show that many kinds of organisms lived at different times in Earth's history. Many species are now extinct. Dinosaurs lived between 65 million and 220 million years ago. There were hundreds of species of dinosaurs. Not one dinosaur lives on Earth today. Saber-toothed cats, giant sloths, giant deer, and tiny shelled animals called trilobites are also examples of extinct animals.

▲ **Figure 4-8** Giant giraffes with antlers once roamed Earth.

Animal bones, shells, and teeth give us clues to past life. So do animal tracks. Another type of fossil that helps us to understand life in the past are animal burrows. These holes or tubes were made by animals in sediment, wood, or rock. They were later filled with sediment and became preserved. Some of the oldest known fossils of this type are worm burrows.

Coprolites are fossilized dung or the stomach contents of ancient animals. Coprolites can tell us what the organisms ate. Some ancient reptiles, including dinosaurs, may have swallowed stones that were used during digestion to grind food. These fossilized stones, which are highly polished, are called **gastroliths.**

▶ 1 LIST: What are four kinds of fossils?

Changes in Living Things Fossils show that plants and animals have changed over time. For example, many fossils of horses have been found. Look at Figure 4-9. These fossils show changes in the animal's size and the number of toes. There was once a four-toed horse about the size of a dog. Fossils of horses also show that changes occurred in their teeth and legs. Today, horses have hooves, not toes, and are fairly large. Other fossils show that modern-day animals such as elephants, giraffes, and camels are related to species that are now extinct.

▶ 2 EXPLAIN: How has the horse changed over millions of years?

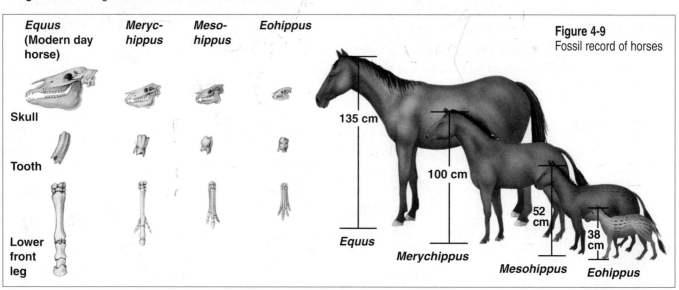

Figure 4-9
Fossil record of horses

Equus (Modern day horse)	Meryc-hippus	Meso-hippus	Eohippus
Skull			
Tooth			
Lower front leg			

135 cm — Equus
100 cm — Merychippus
52 cm — Mesohippus
38 cm — Eohippus

Past Climates and Topography Fossils show that Earth's climate and surface have changed over time. Fossils of alligator-like animals have been found in Canada. Alligators usually live in warm climates. The fossils show that Canada once had a warmer climate than it has today.

Fossils of ferns have been found in Antarctica. These indicate that Antarctica was once very warm. Today, Antarctica is covered with ice and snow. Fossils of coral have been found in Arctic ice.

Fossils of ocean animals have been found in the Andes Mountains in South America. The Andes are 4,000 m above sea level. Scientists believe that the Andes were once under the ocean.

 INFER: How do we know that climates change through the ages?

✔ CHECKING CONCEPTS

Write an E for each extinct organism. Write an N for each living organism.

1. Mammoth
2. Saber-toothed cat
3. Horse
4. Alligator
5. Trilobite
6. Elephant

 THINKING CRITICALLY

7. **ANALYZE:** What do fossils tell us about Earth's surface and climate?
8. **ANALYZE:** What do fossils tell us about living things?

INTERPRETING VISUALS

Use Figure 4-9 to answer the following questions.

9. **OBSERVE:** How many toes did the earliest horses have?
10. **OBSERVE:** Which horse has the largest skull?
11. **ANALYZE:** How has the size of the horse changed over time?

 How Do They Know That?

ANCIENT HUMANLIKE SPECIES

Imagine finding a humanlike skull that is millions of years old. In the late 1950s, the Leakeys did just that. The Leakeys were a family of anthropologists. Anthropologists are scientists who study the history and development of humans and humanlike species.

▲ **Figure 4-10** Mary and Louis Leakey

Mary Leakey and her husband Louis studied fossils for more than 50 years. Much of their work involved looking for fossils of early humans or humanlike species. The Leakeys looked mostly in Tanzania, in the Olduvai Gorge.

In 1959, Mary Leakey found part of a humanlike skull that was more than 1.75 million years old. Over the years, Mary, Louis, and their son Richard found other humanlike fossils. Because he found stone tools at one site, Richard Leakey called the humanlike species he found nearby Handyman.

Louis died in 1972. Mary died in 1996. Richard continues to study fossils.

Thinking Critically What did the Leakeys infer when they found ancient stone tools near the humanlike fossils?

4-3 How do fossils help us date rocks?

Objective
Describe how the relative ages of fossils and rock layers can be determined.

Key Terms
law of superposition: states that each undisturbed sedimentary rock layer is older than the layer above it

relative (REHL-uh-tihv) **age:** age of an object compared to the age of another object

index fossil: fossil used to help determine the relative age of rock layers

Reading Rock Layers Rock sediments are carried from one place and deposited in another by water and wind. These sediments pile up layer upon layer. The bottom layer is deposited first. Each layer is deposited on top of other layers. The sediments are pressed together and harden into sedimentary rock layers that form beds of rock.

The **law of superposition** states that each undisturbed rock layer is older than the layer above it. This law is used by scientists to read rock layers.

Where would you expect to find the oldest layer? Usually, the bottom layer is the oldest layer. The youngest layer is the top layer.

▲ **Figure 4-11** Rock formed in layers will usually follow the law of superposition.

1 OBSERVE: Which rock layer is the youngest in the rock bed illustrated in Figure 4-11?

Relative Age Using the law of superposition, scientists can tell the **relative age** of a rock layer. Relative age is the age of an object compared to the age of another object. Relative age does not tell the exact age of a rock layer.

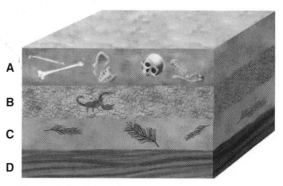

▲ **Figure 4-12** The relative age of a rock layer tells scientists only that one rock layer is older or younger than another rock layer.

2 INFER: What is the relative age of rock layer C in Figure 4-12?

Index Fossils Fossils that can be used to help determine the relative age of rock layers are called **index fossils.** To be an index fossil, a species must have existed for only a short time in Earth's history. Many fossils of this short-lived species need to be recovered from rock layers. These fossils must have a wide geographic range. The fossil organisms must also be unique.

Many kinds of trilobites and graptolites are used as index fossils. Trilobites appeared about 590 million years ago and lived until 250 million years ago. They were small, shelled animals that lived in the ocean. There were many different species of trilobites.

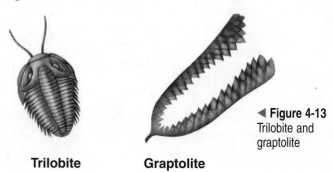

◀ **Figure 4-13** Trilobite and graptolite

Trilobite　　　**Graptolite**

Trilobites had three body parts. They also had a skeleton made of chitin (KY-tihn). Chitin is what your fingernails are made of. If a sedimentary rock contains trilobite fossils, it must have formed between 590 and 250 million years ago, when trilobites were still living. Graptolites appeared about 500 million years ago and lived until 335 million years ago.

Index fossils can also be used to date rock layers from two different parts of the world. Suppose rock layers found in different places contain fossils of the same species of trilobite. Scientists can infer that the layers are about the same age.

 EXPLAIN: What are index fossils used for?

☑ CHECKING CONCEPTS

1. The youngest rock layer is usually the _____ layer.
2. Trilobites are examples of _____ fossils.
3. If one rock layer is older than another, you know the _____ ages of the rock layers.

 THINKING CRITICALLY

4. DESCRIBE: What four qualities make up an index fossil?
5. MODEL: Draw a rock bed with four layers. In one layer, there are 25 trilobite fossils. In another, there are 37 graptolite fossils. The oldest layer is about 600 million years old. Label the oldest and youngest layers and the trilobite and graptolite layers.

BUILDING SCIENCE SKILLS

Modeling Two igneous rock formations can be used to find relative age. These formations are called extrusions and intrusions. They are always younger than the sedimentary rock beds in which they are found. You learned earlier what an extrusion and an intrusion are. Draw a model of a rock bed that has an intrusion and an extrusion. Color the oldest layer in your drawing red. Color the youngest layer yellow.

 Hands-On Activity

MODELING HOW SEDIMENTS ARE DEPOSITED

You will need several different colors of clay, a bowl, and a cheese slicer or plastic knife.

1. Make a stack of different colored layers of clay. Each layer should be about the diameter and thickness of a pancake.
2. Turn the stack into a dome by pressing it over a small rounded object, such as a bowl.
3. With the cheese slicer or plastic knife, carefully slice down from the top and across through the dome so you can see a cross section of the stack. Examine the layers exposed.
4. Push your rock layers close together and then press them down.

▲ STEP 3 Examine the layers you have exposed.

Practicing Your Skills

5. IDENTIFY: Which layer was deposited first?
6. IDENTIFY: Which layer is the oldest?
7. APPLY: How does this model show how sediments are usually deposited?
8. APPLY: Is the oldest layer on the top or the bottom now?

4-4 How is a rock's absolute age determined?

Objectives

Define absolute age in rocks and fossils. Describe ways used to measure it.

Key Terms

absolute age: true age of a rock or fossil

half-life: length of time it takes for one-half the amount of a radioactive element to change into a stable element

Absolute Age To measure your age, you count the number of years from the time you were born. This number is your age. The true age of a rock layer is called its **absolute age.** Absolute age tells scientists the approximate number of years ago a rock layer formed.

1 ▸ DESCRIBE: What is meant by absolute age?

Natural Clocks The process of a radioactive element changing into another element is called radioactive decay. Radioactive elements were first discovered in 1896. They are elements that emit, or give off, particles and energy. As a radioactive element gives off particles and energy, it decays. This causes new elements to form that may or may not be radioactive.

The rate at which radioactive decay happens can be measured. Each radioactive element decays at a regular, steady rate. Radioactive elements are like natural clocks.

2 ▸ EXPLAIN: What is radioactive decay?

Half-life The **half-life** of a radioactive element is the time it takes for one-half of the mass of a sample of a radioactive element to decay. Each radioactive element has a different half-life.

Uranium is a radioactive element. One form of it, called U-238, slowly decays into lead. If you begin with 6 kg of U-238, 3 kg will decay into lead after 4.5 billion years. After another 4.5 billion years, only 1.5 kg of U-238 would be left. By comparing the amount of the radioactive element in a rock to its decay element, scientists can find the absolute age of a rock.

3 ▸ INFER: If a rock has equal amounts of lead and U-238 in it, how old would the rock be?

Carbon-14 Carbon-14 is used to date the remains of living things. As long as living things are alive, they take in carbon-14. Carbon-14 is a radioactive form of carbon. It decays into nitrogen gas. The half-life of carbon-14 is about 5,800 years.

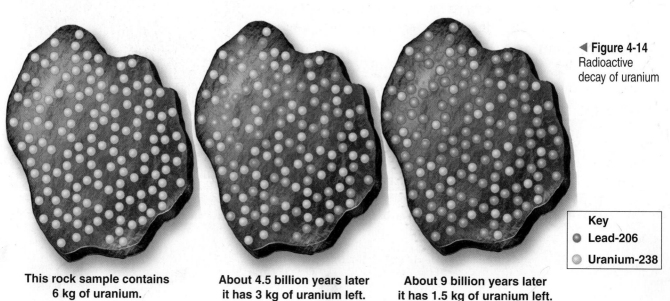

◀ Figure 4-14
Radioactive decay of uranium

Key
● Lead-206
○ Uranium-238

This rock sample contains 6 kg of uranium.

About 4.5 billion years later it has 3 kg of uranium left.

About 9 billion years later it has 1.5 kg of uranium left.

Carbon-14 is used to find out the absolute ages of wood, bones, and so on. It is also used to date "young" samples of fossils. If a sample is more than 50,000 years old, this process cannot be used, since almost all of the carbon-14 has already decayed into nitrogen-14.

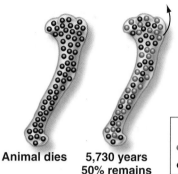

Animal dies   **5,730 years
50% remains**

Key
● Nitrogen-14
● Carbon-14

◄ **Figure 4-15** In the animal bone, the amount of carbon-14 decreases as the carbon-14 decays into the gas nitrogen-14. This gas disperses into the air.

 DESCRIBE: What is carbon-14 used for?

✔ CHECKING CONCEPTS

1. The decay element of U-238 is _____.
2. Radioactive uranium gives off particles and _____.

3. If you read that a fossil is 350–400 billion years old, you are reading its_____ age.
4. The radioactive element _____ is used to find out the absolute age of once-living things.

💡 THINKING CRITICALLY

5. **INFER:** A radioactive element has a half-life of 70 million years. How much of a 10-g sample will be unchanged after 140 million years?
6. **INFER:** Would you use carbon-14 or uranium to find the age of a tooth you think is 20,000 years old? Why?

HEALTH AND SAFETY TIP

Radioactive elements emit radiation. Large amounts of radiation are harmful to living things. Radiation harms cells. Find out what the universal symbol for radiation danger looks like. Draw it on a sheet of paper. What two colors are used in the symbol?

Science and Technology

LASER DATING OF SEDIMENTS

A laser is a very strong, focused beam of light. The light has only one wavelength, or color. You may have several appliances in your house that use laser beams. CD and DVD players use laser beams to read the stored sounds and images on the discs. In Earth science, lasers are used to estimate the age of sediments.

How can lasers be used to estimate the age of sediments? Scientists bombard sediment layers with lasers. The lasers free electrons from the sediments. Electrons are negatively charged particles that can be trapped in sediments. When the electrons are freed, they give off light. Scientists measure how much light is given off. Older sediments give off more electrons than younger sediments do. Laser dating is used to determine the ages of sediments that are up to 700,000 years old. It can also be used to determine the age of river sediments and glacial deposits.

▲ **Figure 4-16** Scientists use lasers to date sediments.

Thinking Critically Why might scientists want to find out the age of glaciers?

4-5 What is the geologic time scale?

INVESTIGATE

Making a Time Line of Your Life
HANDS-ON ACTIVITY

1. List important events that have occurred in your life.
2. Draw a long line across a sheet of paper to represent your life. Break it up into years. You can use a scale of 2 cm for every year.
3. Write each event in the correct year along the time line.
4. Now, divide the time line into parts that describe major periods in your life, such as preschool years, elementary school years, and middle school years.

THINK ABOUT IT: If you had to break up your time line into different groupings or divisions, what might they be?

Objective
Read and interpret the geologic time scale.

Key Term
geologic (jee-uh-LAHJ-ihk) **time scale:** outline of the major divisions in Earth's history

Age of Earth The oldest rocks found on Earth are about 4 billion years old. Moon rocks are older.

Scientists think that Earth and the Moon were formed at about the same time. However, because of the rock cycle, Earth's earliest rocks are gone.

Based on the age of Moon and Earth rocks, scientists think that Earth may be about 4.6 billion years old.

1 DESCRIBE: About how old is Earth?

Outlining Earth's History By studying rocks and fossils, geologists have developed a geologic time scale. The **geologic time scale** outlines the major divisions in Earth's history. It also outlines the kinds of organisms that lived on Earth in the past. The geologic time scale begins when Earth was formed. It continues until the present day.

2 DESCRIBE: What is the geologic time scale?

GEOLOGIC TIME SCALE				
Era	**Period**	**Epoch**	**Approximate Start Date** (millions of years ago)	**Organisms First Appeared**
Cenozoic	Quaternary	Recent	0.025	Modern humans
		Pleistocene	1.75	Mammoths
	Tertiary	Pliocene	14	Large carnivores
		Miocene	26	Many land mammals
		Oligocene	40	Primitive apes
		Eocene	55	Early horses
		Paleocene	65	Primates
Mesozoic	Cretaceous		130	Flowering plants
	Jurassic		180	Dinosaurs
	Triassic		225	Conifers
Paleozoic	Permian		275	Seed plants
	Carboniferous		345	Reptiles
	Devonian		405	Insects, amphibians
	Silurian		435	Fishes
	Ordovician		480	Algae, fungi
	Cambrian		600	Invertebrates
Precambrian			4600	Bacteria, blue-green bacteria

◀ Figure 4-17

Divisions of Geologic Time A year is divided into units called months, weeks, and days. Geologic time is also divided into units. The major unit is an era. Each era in geologic history lasted for millions of years. There are four eras. The eras are divided into periods. The more recent periods are divided into epochs.

The divisions of geologic time are based on important changes that occurred on Earth at these times. Some examples are the extinction of an important group of organisms and afterward the appearance of new categories of animals.

 NAME: What are the divisions of geologic time?

CHECKING CONCEPTS

1. How many eras make up the geologic time scale?
2. How old are the oldest Earth rocks ever found?
3. What does the geologic time scale model?
4. What is the largest unit of geologic time?
5. What is the most recent period of geologic time?

THINKING CRITICALLY

6. **INFER:** Why are only the most recent periods divided into epochs?
7. **HYPOTHESIZE:** If the oldest Earth rocks are only 4 billion years old, why do scientists think that Earth is 4.6 billion years old?

BUILDING SCIENCE SKILLS

Modeling Use adding machine tape to make your own timeline. Have each centimeter equal 10 million years. Calculate the length of each era in centimeters. Draw lines on the tape to mark each era. Mark each of the events listed below. Add five other events to your timeline using Figure 4-17.

- First fossils appeared 3.4 billion years ago.
- First fish appeared 450 million years ago.
- First reptiles appeared 290 million years ago.
- Age of dinosaurs began 200 million years ago.
- First mammals appeared 200 million years ago.
- First birds appeared 150 million years ago.
- First humanlike animals appeared 2 million years ago.
- Last major ice age ended 10,000 years ago.

Integrating Life Science

TOPICS: extinction, biodiversity

THE DIVERSITY OF LIFE

Earth is teeming with life. However, scientists estimate that for every species existing today, at least 100 others are now extinct.

Earth has changed greatly over its history. Mountains have been built up. Volcanoes have formed. There have been ice ages. The Sun's output has varied over time. Each time a great change has occurred, species that could not adapt died out. Others replaced them. Today, Earth may have up to 100 million species.

▲ **Figure 4-18** An asteroid striking Earth is believed to have led to the extinction of the dinosaurs.

Scientists call this vast variety of organisms biodiversity. Together, the various species keep natural cycles, such as the water and nitrogen cycles, running smoothly. Each species helps balance the ecosystem of which it is a part. For example, some species break down wastes. Others add oxygen to the air. The loss of even a few species can result in the destruction of an ecosystem.

Thinking Critically How do pollution and the spread of civilization threaten biodiversity?

4-6 What are fossil fuels?

Objective
Describe how coal, oil, and natural gas were formed.

Key Term
fossil fuel (FYOO-uhl): natural fuel that was formed from the remains of living things

Fossils as Fuel A fuel is a substance that gives off energy when it is burned. A fuel may be a solid, liquid, or gas. **Fossil fuels** are fuels that were formed from fossils.

Coal and natural gas are fossil fuels. The liquid fuel known as petroleum is also a fossil fuel. Most of the energy that heats our homes and runs our appliances comes from fossil fuels.

▶ **1 DEFINE:** What are the fossil fuels?

Hydrocarbons Fossil fuels are made up mostly of hydrocarbons. Hydrocarbons are compounds made up of the elements hydrogen and carbon. Hydrocarbons store energy. This energy comes from the sunlight absorbed by plants and microorganisms that lived millions of years ago. When hydrocarbons are burned, they give off this energy as light and heat.

▶ **2 IDENTIFY:** What two forms of energy are given off when hydrocarbons are burned?

The Formation of Coal Coal is formed in swamps. Swamps are areas of shallow water with a lot of plant life. When the plants in the swamps die, they are covered by water and by sediments such as mud. Bacteria, pressure, and heat slowly cause chemical changes to take place in the plants. After many millions of years, the decaying plant material changes to peat. Peat is the first stage in coal formation. After another long period of time, peat changes into soft coal. Pressure changes soft coal into hard coal. Soft and hard coal are mostly carbon. They give off a lot of heat when they burn.

▶ **3 NAME:** What are the three basic stages of coal formation?

The Formation of Oil and Natural Gas Geologists think that petroleum, or crude oil, and natural gas were formed from decaying microorganisms. When these microorganisms died, they were covered with sediments that became sedimentary rock.

Like coal, petroleum and natural gas were formed by the actions of bacteria, heat, and pressure. Petroleum moved with water through the cracks and pores in rock. When it reached a rock layer it could not pass through, the mixture of petroleum and water began to collect. Petroleum is usually found in pools that collect in layers of shale or sandstone. The petroleum floats on top of the water.

▲ **Figure 4-19** During the coal-forming age, much of Earth was covered by huge swamps.

If natural gas is also present, it is on top of the oil. To get to the oil and natural gas, it is necessary to drill into Earth's crust.

 4 NAME: What types of ancient organisms formed oil and natural gas?

✓ CHECKING CONCEPTS

1. What compounds are found in fossil fuels?

2. What are three fossil fuels?

3. What three things act on decaying organisms to help form fossil fuels?

4. In what kind of rock layers would you most likely find petroleum and natural gas?

💡 THINKING CRITICALLY

5. INFER: Why are coal, petroleum, and natural gas called fossil fuels?

6. IDENTIFY: What is the source of the energy stored in hydrocarbons?

7. INFER: Why is natural gas found above petroleum in an oil deposit?

INTERPRETING VISUALS

A pictograph is a graph that uses a picturelike symbol to show an idea. Use the pictograph below to do the following exercises.

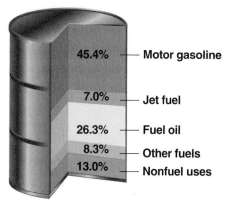

45.4%	Motor gasoline
7.0%	Jet fuel
26.3%	Fuel oil
8.3%	Other fuels
13.0%	Nonfuel uses

▲ **Figure 4-20** Uses of Petroleum

8. Place the uses of petroleum in order from greatest use to least use.

9. Give the percentage of petroleum that is used to make all fuels.

10. What total percentage of petroleum fuel goes toward transportation needs?

 People in Science

OIL-RIG OPERATOR

An oil-rig operator often works at sea. The drilling structure is a tall steel frame called a jacket. It is built onshore and carried out to sea on a barge. Then, it is anchored to the seafloor. The machines used to extract the oil are on a platform on top of the jacket. The construction crew sets the derrick, which holds the drilling equipment, over the spot where the well is to be drilled.

The workers live on the platform. They may be away from home for up to three weeks at a time. They run the drill, pumps, power plant, and control room. The drilling crew changes bits that are dull or cannot penetrate the rock. Most drilling crews have one driller, one or more derrickmen, and several other workers. Many oil-rig workers start out as roustabouts. Roustabouts do the heavy, unskilled labor. Many companies train roustabouts to do more skilled work.

Oil-rig workers must be physically fit. They must also usually take what is called the Basic Offshore Survival and Firefighting training course. This lasts for 2½ days.

Thinking Critically What kind of labor might roustabouts do?

▲ **Figure 4-21** An oil rig in operation off the coast of California

THE Big IDEA

What products are made from oil?

It might not seem like crayons, guitar strings, footballs, and bubble gum have anything in common, but they do. Each of these products is made from crude oil.

Ancient peoples recognized the value of this natural resource. The Chinese used oil to waterproof their homes. Egyptians wrapped their dead in rags saturated with oil to preserve them. Native Americans added a drop or two of oil to medicines, and ancient Romans applied oil to cuts and wounds. Thanks to technology, today there are more than 500,000 different uses for this natural resource.

The first step in creating these products is separating crude oil into its different parts. This is called fractional distillation and takes place in an oil refinery. Pipes carry raw crude oil from oil wells to the refinery. The crude oil is heated to about 430°C. This causes the liquid to turn into vapor. The vapor is then pumped into a tall tower divided into different levels. Each of these levels is kept at a certain temperature.

As the evaporated crude oil moves through the tower, its substances condense at different temperatures. The heaviest parts condense in the warmer, lower levels of the tower. The lightest parts condense in the cooler, higher levels of the tower. The separated substances are drawn from each level and sent to other locations, where they are used to make many products.

Look at the illustrations on these two pages. Then, follow the directions in the Science Log to learn more about "the big idea." ✦

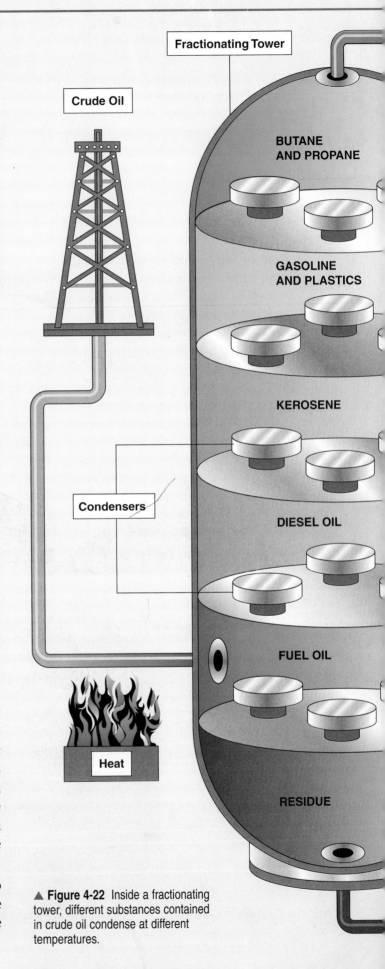

▲ **Figure 4-22** Inside a fractionating tower, different substances contained in crude oil condense at different temperatures.

Butane and Propane

The lightest parts of evaporated crude oil condense in the coolest level of the tower. Butane used in lighters and propane used in barbecue grills are collected here.

Kerosene

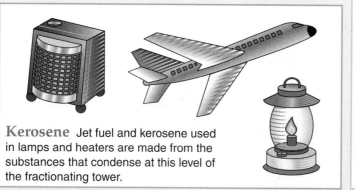

Kerosene Jet fuel and kerosene used in lamps and heaters are made from the substances that condense at this level of the fractionating tower.

Gasoline and Plastics

The gasoline that cars run on comes from substances that condense in this level. Chemicals and plastics used to make clothing, sporting equipment, and telephones start at this level.

Diesel Oil Trucks and trains run on diesel fuel made from substances that condense at this level.

Fuel Oil Heating oil is used to keep many homes warm. Certain fuels power ships and factories. All are made from substances that condense at this level.

Residue Lubricants, paraffin, and asphalt are made from the residues that condense in the lowest level of the tower.

WRITING ACTIVITY

Science Log

List all of the crude oil products that you have used this week. Name at least five. Then, write several paragraphs entitled "A Day Without Oil Products." Describe in these paragraphs what your day would be like without these items. Start your search for information using www.conceptsandchallenges.com.

Chapter 4 Challenges

Chapter Summary

Lesson 4-1

- **Fossils** are the remains or traces of organisms that lived many years ago.
- Fossils form in sedimentary rock. Members of some extinct species have been preserved in frozen soil or ice.
- The bones of many animals trapped in tar pits were preserved.
- Some insects and plant parts have been perfectly preserved in **amber.**

Lesson 4-2

- Fossils show that many kinds of organisms lived at different times in Earth's history. They show that some living things have changed over millions of years. They also show that Earth's climate and surface have changed over million of years.

Lesson 4-3

- Scientists use the **law of superposition** to tell the **relative age** of a rock layer.
- **Index fossils** can be used to help find the relative age of rock layers in the same area or from two different parts of the world.

Lesson 4-4

- The specific age of a rock or a fossil is called its **absolute age.**
- Radioactive elements are like natural clocks. The **half-life** of radioactive elements can be used to find the absolute age of a rock or fossil.
- Carbon-14 is used to find the absolute age of the remains of living things.

Lesson 4-5

- Some scientists estimate that Earth is more than 4.6 billion years old.
- The **geologic time scale** is a record of the major divisions in Earth's history.
- The major divisions of geologic time are eras, periods, and epochs.

Lesson 4-6

- Petroleum, coal, and natural gas are **fossil fuels.**
- When hydrocarbons are burned, they give off energy as light and heat.

Key Term Challenges

absolute age (p. 98)
amber (p. 90)
cast (p. 90)
coprolite (p. 94)
fossil (p. 90)
fossil fuel (p. 102)
gastrolith (p. 94)
geologic time scale (p. 100)
half-life (p. 98)
index fossil (p. 96)
law of superposition (p. 96)
mold (p. 90)
relative age (p. 96)

MATCHING Write the Key Term from above that best matches each description.

1. outline of the major divisions in Earth's history

2. imprint in a rock that has the shape of an extinct organism

3. age of an object compared to the age of another object

4. specific age of a rock or fossil

5. length of time it takes for one-half the amount of a radioactive element to change into another element

FILL IN Write the Key Term from above that best completes each statement.

6. Oil, coal, and natural gas are three kinds of _____.

7. A mold that has been filled with sediments forms a _____.

8. The bodies of entire insects have been found preserved in hardened tree sap called _____.

9. The traces or remains of living things that lived long ago are called _____.

10. A trilobite can be used as an _____.

11. A _____ was a stone some ancient animals swallowed to help grind up their food.

12. Scientists use the _____ to tell the relative age of rocks and fossils.

Content Challenges TEST PREP

MULTIPLE CHOICE Write the letter of the term or phrase that best completes each statement.

1. A species that once lived on Earth but is no longer found alive is called
   a. a fossil.
   b. an imprint.
   c. a cast.
   d. extinct.

2. Most fossils are found in
   a. metamorphic rock.
   b. sedimentary rock.
   c. mud.
   d. igneous rock.

3. Footprints are a kind of fossil called
   a. a mold.
   b. a cast.
   c. an imprint.
   d. amber.

4. The bodies of wooly mammoths and wooly rhinoceroses have been found preserved in
   a. amber.
   b. sedimentary rocks.
   c. ice.
   d. petrified forests.

5. Three ways in which the entire bodies of organisms are preserved are
   a. ice, tar, and amber.
   b. ice, molds, and casts.
   c. tar, molds, and casts.
   d. molds, petrified wood, and amber.

6. Graptolites and trilobites are two kinds of
   a. radioactive elements.
   b. molds.
   c. casts.
   d. index fossils.

7. Peat is the first stage in the formation of
   a. natural gas.
   b. tar.
   c. coal.
   d. petroleum.

8. The law of superposition states that each undisturbed rock layer is older than the one
   a. beside it.
   b. above it.
   c. below it.
   d. to its left.

9. Fossils show how Earth's climate and topography have
   a. changed over time.
   b. stayed about the same over time.
   c. improved over time.
   d. worsened over time.

TRUE/FALSE Write *true* if the statement is true. If the statement is false, change the underlined term to make the statement true.

10. Shells and <u>nails</u> are often the only parts of organisms that are preserved.

11. Elephant-like animals called <u>saber-toothed cats</u> have been discovered preserved in ice.

12. The LaBrea tar pits are located in southern <u>California</u>.

13. The bodies of entire insects have been found preserved in <u>amber</u>.

14. When fossil fuels are burned, they give off energy in the forms of heat and <u>electricity</u>.

15. Fossil fuels are formed when <u>bacteria</u>, heat, and pressure act on decaying plants and animals.

16. Fossils of alligator-like animals found in Canada indicate that the climate of Canada was <u>always cold</u>.

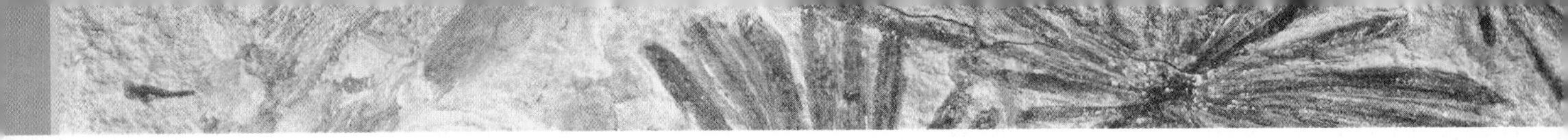

Concept Challenges TEST PREP

WRITTEN RESPONSE Answer each of the following questions in complete sentences.

1. **INFER:** Suppose you find fossils of clams in rock high on a mountain. What can you infer about the mountain?

2. **DESCRIBE:** How is U-238 used for the specific dating of rocks?

3. **DESCRIBE:** What is the geologic time scale? Give examples in your explanation.

4. **EXPLAIN:** Why is carbon-14 not useful for dating rocks that are more than 50,000 years old?

5. **ANALYZE:** What method would you use to date a sedimentary rock that you think is about 1 million years old? Why?

INTERPRETING VISUALS Use Figure 4-23 to answer the following questions.

6. What is the name of the most recent era in geologic time?

7. How long ago did dinosaurs roam Earth's surface?

8. During which period did conifers such as pine trees first appear?

9. During which period did snakes first appear?

10. Which era lasted the longest?

GEOLOGIC TIME SCALE				
Era	**Period**	**Epoch**	**Approximate Start Date** (millions of years ago)	**Organisms First Appeared**
Cenozoic	Quaternary	Recent	0.025	Modern humans
		Pleistocene	1.75	Mammoths
	Tertiary	Pliocene	14	Large carnivores
		Miocene	26	Many land mammals
		Oligocene	40	Primitive apes
		Eocene	55	Early horses
		Paleocene	65	Primates
Mesozoic	Cretaceous		130	Flowering plants
	Jurassic		180 	Dinosaurs
	Triassic		225	Conifers
Paleozoic	Permian		275	Seed plants
	Carboniferous		345	Reptiles
	Devonian		405	Insects, amphibians
	Silurian		435	Fishes
	Ordovician		480	Algae, fungi
	Cambrian		600 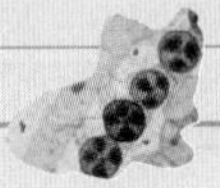	Invertebrates
Precambrian			4600	Bacteria, blue-green bacteria

▲ Figure 4-23

Appendix A Metric System

The Metric System and SI Units

The metric system is an international system of measurement based on units of ten. More than 90% of the nations of the world use the metric system. In the United States, both the English system and the metric system are used.

The *Système International*, or SI, has been used as the international measurement system since 1960. The SI is a modernized version of the metric system. Like the metric system, the SI is a decimal system based on units of ten. When you want to change from one unit in the metric system to another unit, you multiply or divide by a multiple of ten.

- When you change from a smaller unit to a larger unit, you divide.

- When you change from a larger unit to a smaller unit, you multiply.

COMMON METRIC PREFIXES

micro-	0.000001 or 1/1,000,000	deka-	10
milli-	0.001 or 1/1,000	hecto-	100
centi-	0.01 or 1/100	kilo-	1,000
deci-	0.1 or 1/10	mega-	1,000,000

▲ Figure 2

METRIC UNITS

LENGTH	SYMBOL	RELATIONSHIP
kilometer	km	1 km = 1,000 m
meter	m	1 m = 100 cm
centimeter	cm	1 cm = 10 mm
millimeter	mm	1 mm = 0.1 cm
AREA	SYMBOL	
square kilometer	km^2	$1\ km^2 = 1,000,000\ m^2$
square meter	m^2	$1\ m^2 = 1,000,000\ mm^2$
square centimeter	cm^2	$1\ cm^2 = 0.0001\ m^2$
square millimeter	mm^2	$1\ mm^2 = 0.000001\ m^2$
VOLUME	SYMBOL	
cubic meter	m^3	$1\ m^3 = 1,000,000\ cm^3$
cubic centimeter	cm^3	$1\ cm^3 = 0.000001\ m^3$
liter	L	1 L = 1,000 mL
milliliter	mL	1 mL = 0.001 L
MASS	SYMBOL	
metric ton	t	1 t = 1,000 kg
kilogram	kg	1 kg = 1,000 g
gram	g	1 g = 1,000 mg
centigram	cg	1 cg = 10 mg
milligram	mg	1 mg = 0.001 g
TEMPERATURE	SYMBOL	
Kelvin	K	
degree Celsius	°C	

▲ Figure 1

METRIC-STANDARD EQUIVALENTS

SI to English	English to SI
LENGTH	
1 kilometer = 0.621 mile (mi)	1 mi = 1.61 km
1 meter = 1.094 yards (yd)	1 yd = 0.914 m
1 meter = 3.28 feet (ft)	1 ft = 0.305 m
1 centimeter = 0.394 inch (in.)	1 in. = 2.54 cm
1 millimeter = 0.039 inch	1 in. = 25.4 mm
AREA	
1 square kilometer = 0.3861 square mile	$1\ mi^2 = 2.590\ km^2$
1 square meter = 1.1960 square yards	$1\ yd^2 = 0.8361\ m^2$
1 square meter = 10.763 square feet	$1\ ft^2 = 0.0929\ m^2$
1 square centimeter = 0.155 square inch	$1\ in.^2 = 6.452\ cm^2$
VOLUME	
1 cubic meter = 1.3080 cubic yards	$1\ yd^3 = 0.7646\ m^3$
1 cubic meter = 35.315 cubic feet	$1\ ft^3 = 0.0283\ m^3$
1 cubic centimeter = 0.0610 cubic inch	$1\ in.^3 = 16.39\ cm^3$
1 liter = 0.2642 gallon (gal)	1 gal = 3.79 L
1 liter = 1.06 quarts (qt)	1 qt = 0.946 L
1 liter = 2.11 pints (pt)	1 pt = 0.47 L
1 milliliter = 0.034 fluid ounce (fl oz)	1 fl oz = 29.57 mL
MASS	
1 metric ton = 0.984 ton	1 ton = 1.016 t
1 kilogram = 2.205 pounds (lb)	1 lb = 0.4536 kg
1 gram = 0.0353 ounce (oz)	1 oz = 28.35 g
TEMPERATURE	
Celsius = 5/9(°F − 32)	Fahrenheit = 9/5°C + 32
0°C = 32°F (Freezing point of water)	72°F = 22°C (Room temperature)
100°C = 212°F (Boiling point of water)	98.6°F = 37°C (Human body temperature)
Kelvin = (°F + 459.67)/1.8	Fahrenheit = (K × 1.8) − 459.67

▲ Figure 3

Appendix B Chemical Elements

LIST OF CHEMICAL ELEMENTS

Element	Atomic Symbol	Atomic Number
Actinium	Ac	89
Aluminum	Al	13
Americium	Am	95
Antimony	Sb	51
Argon	Ar	18
Arsenic	As	33
Astatine	At	85
Barium	Ba	56
Berkelium	Bk	97
Beryllium	Be	4
Bismuth	Bi	83
Bohrium	Bh	107
Boron	B	5
Bromine	Br	35
Cadmium	Cd	48
Calcium	Ca	20
Californium	Cf	98
Carbon	C	6
Cerium	Ce	58
Cesium	Cs	55
Chlorine	Cl	17
Chromium	Cr	24
Cobalt	Co	27
Copper	Cu	29
Curium	Cm	96
Dubnium	Db	105
Dysprosium	Dy	66
Einsteinium	Es	99
Erbium	Er	68
Europium	Eu	63
Fermium	Fm	100
Fluorine	F	9
Francium	Fr	87
Gadolinium	Gd	64
Gallium	Ga	31
Germanium	Ge	32
Gold	Au	79

▲ Figure 4

LIST OF CHEMICAL ELEMENTS

Element	Atomic Symbol	Atomic Number
Hafnium	Hf	72
Hassium	Hs	108
Helium	He	2
Holmium	Ho	67
Hydrogen	H	1
Indium	In	49
Iodine	I	53
Iridium	Ir	77
Iron	Fe	26
Krypton	Kr	36
Lanthanum	La	57
Lawrencium	Lr	103
Lead	Pb	82
Lithium	Li	3
Lutetium	Lu	71
Magnesium	Mg	12
Manganese	Mn	25
Meitnerium	Mt	109
Mendelevium	Md	101
Mercury	Hg	80
Molybdenum	Mo	42
Neodymium	Nd	60
Neon	Ne	10
Neptunium	Np	93
Nickel	Ni	28
Niobium	Nb	41
Nitrogen	N	7
Nobelium	No	102
Osmium	Os	76
Oxygen	O	8
Palladium	Pd	46
Phosphorus	P	15
Platinum	Pt	78
Plutonium	Pu	94
Polonium	Po	84
Potassium	K	19
Praseodymium	Pr	59
Promethium	Pm	61

LIST OF CHEMICAL ELEMENTS

Element	Atomic Symbol	Atomic Number
Protactinium	Pa	91
Radium	Ra	88
Radon	Rn	86
Rhenium	Re	75
Rhodium	Rh	45
Rubidium	Rb	37
Ruthenium	Ru	44
Rutherfordium	Rf	104
Samarium	Sm	62
Scandium	Sc	21
Seaborgium	Sg	106
Selenium	Se	34
Silicon	Si	14
Silver	Ag	47
Sodium	Na	11
Strontium	Sr	38
Sulfur	S	16
Tantalum	Ta	73
Technetium	Tc	43
Tellurium	Te	52
Terbium	Tb	65
Thallium	Tl	81
Thorium	Th	90
Thulium	Tm	69
Tin	Sn	50
Titanium	Ti	22
Tungsten	W	74
Ununnilium	Uun	110
Unununium	Uuu	111
Ununbium	Uub	112
Ununquadium	Uuq	114
Uranium	U	92
Vanadium	V	23
Xenon	Xe	54
Ytterbium	Yb	70
Yttrium	Y	39
Zinc	Zn	30
Zirconium	Zr	40

Appendix C Science Terms

Analyzing Science Terms

You can often unlock the meaning of an unfamiliar science term by analyzing its word parts. Prefixes and suffixes, for example, each carry a meaning that comes from a word root. This word root usually comes from the Latin or Greek language. The following list of prefixes and suffixes provides clues to the meaning of many science terms.

WORD PART	MEANING	EXAMPLE
astr-, aster-	star	astronomy
bar-, baro-	weight, pressure	barometer
batho-, bathy-	depth	batholith, bathysphere
circum-	around	circum-Pacific, circumpolar
-cline	lean, slope	anticline, syncline
eco-	environment	ecology, ecosystem
epi-	on	epicenter
ex-, exo-	out, outside of	exosphere, exfoliation, extrusion
geo-	earth	geode, geology, geomagnetic
-graph	write, writing	seismograph
hydro-	water	hydrosphere
hypo-	under	hypothesis
iso-	equal	isoscope, isostasy, isotope
-lith, -lithic	stone	Neolithic, regolith
magn-	great, large	magnitude
mar-	sea	marine
meso-	middle	mesosphere, Mesozoic
meta-	among, change	metamorphic, metamorphism
micro-	small	microquake
-morph, -morphic	form	metamorphic
neo-	new	Neolithic
paleo-	old	paleontology, Paleozoic
ped-, pedo-	ground, soil	pediment
peri-	around	perigee, perihelion
-ose	carbohydrate	glucose, cellulose
seism-, seismo-	shake, earthquake	seismic, seismograph
sol-	sun	solar, solstice
spectro-	look at, examine	spectroscope, spectrum
-sphere	ball, globe	hemisphere, lithosphere
strati-, strato-	spread, layer	stratification, stratovolcano
terra-	earth, land	terracing, terrane
thermo-	heat	thermosphere
top-, topo-	place	topographic
tropo-	turn, respond to	tropopause, troposphere

▲ Figure 5

Appendix D Guide to Common Rocks and Minerals

COMMON ROCKS		
Rock Name	**Rock Type**	**Comments**
Anthracite coal	Sedimentary	Dark brown to black in color; shiny, hard, scaly, and dense; used as fuel; also used in producing coal gas and in the iron, steel, synthetic rubber, and dye industries
Basalt	Igneous	Fine-grained; dark in color; often rings like a bell when struck with a hammer; used for road paving
Compact limestone	Sedimentary	Fine-grained, soft, and porous; normally pale in color; used in building stones and in making lime
Conglomerate	Sedimentary	Very colorful; texture varies; consists of pebbles cemented together; often contains useful mineral grains; used as a building stone
Gneiss	Metamorphic	Coarse-grained; layers of different minerals often give a banded appearance; some varieties used as building material, both rough and polished
Granite	Igneous	Coarse-grained; mostly light in color, in shades of pink, gray, and white; important building stone, either polished or rough
Marble	Metamorphic	Coarse-grained; reacts with acid; color varies; often patterned; important building stone
Mica schist	Metamorphic	Medium- to coarse-grained; sparkly gray to black in color; contains important minerals
Obsidian	Igneous	Light to dark in color; glassy luster; sometimes translucent; brittle; used industrially as raw material; in ancient times was used for tools and sculptures
Pumice	Igneous	Light to dark in color; spongy appearance; many holes; lightweight, may float in water; used as building insulation
Sandstone	Sedimentary	Coarse-grained; usually sand color; often contains deposits of oil and gas; used for building
Shale	Sedimentary	Microscopic grains; clay composition; smooth surface, hardened mud appearance; some varieties, when processed, yield oil
Slate	Metamorphic	Find-grained; cleaves into thin flat plates; shiny dark gray color; used as shingles for roofing, for flooring, and blackboards

▲ Figure 6

MINERALS			
Mineral	Chemical Formula	Color	Streak
Apatite	$Ca_5(F,Cl)(PO_4)_3$	Green, brown, red	White
Augite	$Ca(Mg, Fe, Al)(Al, Si_2O_6)$	Dark green, black	Green to gray
Beryl	$Be_3Al_2Si_6O_{18}$	White, yellow, blue, green	White
Biotite (Mica)	Complex substance containing Fe, Mg, Si, O and other elements	Black, brown, dark green	White to light brown
Calcite	$CaCO_3$	Gray, white	White
Chalcopyrite	$CuFeS_2$	Brass, yellow	Greenish black
Copper	Cu	Copper red to black	Copper red
Corundum	Al_2O_3	Various colors	White
Diamond	C	Colorless to black	Colorless
Dolomite	$CaMg(CO_3)_2$	Pink, white, gray, green, brown, black	White
Feldspar	$(K, NA, CA)(AlSi_3O_8)$	Colorless, white, various colors	Colorless, white
Fluorite	CaF_2	Light green yellow, bluish green, and other colors	White
Galena	PbS	Lead gray	Lead gray
Gold	Au	Gold	Gold
Graphite	C	Black to gray	Black
Gypsum	$CaSO_4 \cdot 2H_2O$	Whitish gray	White
Halite	NaCl	Colorless and various colors	Colorless
Hematite	Fe_2O_3	Reddish brown to black	Light to dark red
Hornblende	Complex substance containing Ca, Na, Mg, Ti, and Al	Dark green, black, brown	Colorless
Magnetite	Fe_4O_4	Iron black	Black
Olivine	$(Mg,Fe)_2SiO_4$	Olive green	White
Pyrite	FeS_2	Brass, yellow	Greenish, brownish, black
Quartz	SiO_2	Colorless, white, any color when not pure	White
Serpentine	$Mg_3Si_2O_5(OH)_4$	Green, yellow, brown, or black	White
Silver	Ag	Silver, black	Silver
Sphalerite	ZnS	Brown, black, red, and other colors	White, yellow, brown
Sulfur	S	Yellow	White
Talc	$Mg_3Si_4O_{10}(OH)_2$	Gray, greenish white	White

▲ Figure 7

MINERALS				
Mineral	Luster*	Hardness	Specific Gravity	Fracture/Cleavage
Apatite	Vitreous	5	3.1–3.2	Fracture
Augite	Vitreous	5–6	3.2–3.6	Cleavage
Beryl	Vitreous	8	2.65–2.90	Cleavage
Biotite (Mica)	Vitreous	2.5–6	2.8–3.2	Cleavage
Calcite	Vitreous	3	2.7	Cleavage
Chalcopyrite	Metallic	3.5–4	4.1–4.34	Fracture
Copper	Metallic	2.5–3	8.5–8.93	None
Corundum	Vitreous to adamantine	9	4.02	Cleavage
Diamond	Adamantine	10	3.52	Cleavage
Dolomite	Vitreous to pearly	3.5–4	2.85	Cleavage
Feldspar	Vitreous	6	2.55–2.75	Cleavage
Fluorite	Vitreous	4	3.18	Cleavage
Galena	Metallic	2.5	7.4–7.6	Cleavage
Gold	Metallic	2.5–3	15.3–19.3	None
Graphite	Metallic	1–2	2.3	Cleavage
Gypsum	Silky	2	2.3–2.4	Cleavage
Halite	Vitreous	2.5	2.1–2.6	Cleavage
Hematite	Metallic	5–6	5.26	Fracture
Hornblende	Vitreous	5–6	3.2	Cleavage
Magnetite	Metallic	6	5.18	Fracture
Olivine	Vitreous	6.5–7	3.2–4.2	Fracture
Pyrite	Metallic	6–6.5	4.9–5.2	Fracture
Quartz	Vitreous	7	2.65	Fracture
Serpentine	Vitreous	2–5	2.5–3.2	Fracture
Silver	Metallic	2.5–3	10.0–12.0	None
Sphalerite	Metallic, submetallic, adamantine, resinous	3.5–4	3.9–4.1	Cleavage
Sulfur	Adamantine	1.5–2.5	2.0–2.1	Cleavage
Talc	Vitreous	1	2.7–2.8	Cleavage

*Luster is the appearance of the light reflected from the surface of a mineral. This is another aid to identifying minerals. Adamantine describes a mineral that has a brilliant diamondlike luster. Vitreous describes a mineral that has a glassy luster.

▲ Figure 8

Glossary

Pronunciation and syllabication have been derived from *Webster's New World Dictionary*, Second College Edition, Revised School Printing (Prentice Hall, 1985). Syllables printed in capital letters are given primary stress. (Numbers in parentheses indicate the page number, or page numbers, on which the term is defined.)

PRONUNCIATION KEY					
Symbol	Example	Respelling	Symbol	Example	Respelling
a	transpiration	(tran-spuh-RAY-shuhn)	oh	biome	(BY-ohm)
ah	composite	(kuhm-PAHZ-iht)	oi	asteroid	(AS-tuhr-oid)
aw	atoll	(A-tawl)	oo	altitude	(AL-tuh-tood)
ay	abrasion	(uh-BRAY-zhuhn)	ow	compound	(KAHM-pownd)
ch	leaching	(LEECH-ing)	s	satellite	(SAT-uhl-yt)
eh	chemical	(KEHM-i-kuhl)	sh	specialization	(spehsh-uhl-ih-ZAY-shuhn)
ee	equinox	(EE-kwih-nahks)	th	thermocline	(THUR-muh-klyn)
f	hemisphere	(HEHM-ih-sfeer)	th	weathering	(WEHTH-uhr-ing)
g	galaxy	(GAL-uhk-see)	uh	volcanism	(VAHL-kuh-nihzm)
ih	anticline	(AN-tih-klyn)	y, eye	anticline, isobar	(AN-tih-klyn), (EYE-soh-bahr)
j	geologic	(jee-uh-LAHJ-ihk)	yoo	cumulus	(KYOOM-yuh-luhs)
k	current	(KUR-uhnt)	z	deposition	(dehp-uh-ZIHSH-uhn)
ks	axis	(AK-sihs)	zh	erosion	(e-ROH-zhuhn)

absolute age: true age of a rock or fossil (p. 98)

acid test: test that helps to identify minerals containing calcium carbonate (p. 50)

amber: hardened tree sap (p. 90)

atmosphere (AT-muhs-feer): envelope of gases that surrounds Earth (p. 18)

atom: smallest part of an element that can be identified as that element (p. 42)

cast: mold filled with hardened sediments (p. 90)

chemical (KEHM-ih-kuhl) **formula:** formula that shows the elements that make up a compound (p. 44)

chemical symbol: shorthand way of writing the name of an element (p. 44)

clastic (KLAS-tihk) **rock:** sedimentary rock made up of fragments of rock (p. 74)

cleavage (KLEEV-ihj): tendency of some minerals to split along smooth, flat surfaces called planes (p. 52)

communication: sharing information (p. 8)

compound (KAHM-pownd): substance made up of two or more elements that are chemically combined (p. 42)

constant: something that does not change (p. 11)

contour interval (KAHN-toor IHN-tuhr-vuhl): difference in elevation between one contour line and the next (p. 34)

contour line: line drawn on a map that connects all points having the same elevation (p. 32)

controlled experiment: experiment in which all the conditions except one are kept constant (p. 11)

coprolite (KAHP-roh-lyt): fossil dung or the stomach contents of ancient animals (p. 94)

core: innermost region of Earth (p. 20)

crust: solid, thin outer layer of Earth (p. 20)

crystal (KRIHS-tuhl): solid substance with its atoms arranged in a regular three-dimensional pattern (p. 52)

crystallization: formation of minerals caused by processes such as cooling and evaporation (p. 54)

cycle: series of events that happen over and over again (p. 80)

data: information you collect when you observe something (p. 3)

density (DEHN-suh-tee): amount of matter in a given volume (p. 50)

distortion (dih-STAWR-shuhn): error in shape, size, or distance (p. 22)

Earth science: study of Earth and its history (p. 16)

element (EHL-uh-muhnt): simple substance that cannot be broken down into simpler substances by ordinary chemical means (p. 42)

elevation (ehl-uh-VAY-shuhn): height of a point on Earth above or below sea level (p. 32)

equator: imaginary line that runs around the middle of Earth's surface and divides it into the Northern and Southern hemispheres (p. 26)

evaporation (ee-vap-uh-RAY-shuhn): process by which a liquid changes into a gas (p. 54)

foliated (FOH-lee-ayt-uhd): texture of a metamorphic rock that has mineral crystals arranged in bands (p. 78)

fossil (FAHS-uhl): remains or traces of an organism that lived long ago (p. 90)

fossil fuel (FYOO-uhl): natural fuel that was formed from the remains of living things (p. 102)

fracture (FRAK-chuhr): tendency of some minerals to break into pieces with uneven surfaces (p. 52)

gastrolith (GAS-troh-lihth): stone used to grind food (p. 94)

gem: stone that has been cut and polished (p. 58)

geologic (jee-uh-LAHJ-ihk) **time scale:** outline of the major divisions in Earth's history (p. 100)

globe: three-dimensional model of Earth's surface (p. 22)

gram: basic unit of mass (p. 4)

half-life: length of time it takes for one-half the amount of a radioactive element to change into a stable element (p. 98)

hardness: property of a mineral that relates to how much the mineral resists being scratched (p. 48)

hemisphere (HEHM-ih-sfeer): one-half of a sphere (p. 26)

hydrosphere (HY-droh-sfeer): part of Earth that is water (p. 18)

hypothesis: suggested answer to a question or problem (p. 10)

igneous (IHG-nee-uhs) **rock:** rock formed by the crystallization of hot melted rocks or minerals (p. 66)

index fossil: fossil used to help determine the relative age of rock layers (p. 96)

latitude (LAT-uh-tood): distance north or south of the equator in degrees (p. 26)

lava (LAH-vuh): magma that reaches Earth's surface (p. 68)

law of superposition: states that each undisturbed sedimentary rock layer is older than the layer above it (p. 96)

legend (LEHJ-uhnd): list of map symbols and their meanings (p. 28)

liter: basic unit of liquid volume (p. 4)

lithosphere (LIHTH-oh-sfeer): solid part of Earth (p. 18)

longitude (LAHN-juh-tood): measurement in degrees east or west of the prime meridian (p. 26)

luster: how a mineral's surface reflects light (p. 48)

magma (MAG-muh): molten rock inside Earth (p. 68)

magnetism (MAG-nuh-tihz-uhm): force of attraction or repulsion associated with magnets (p. 50)

mantle (MAN-tuhl): thick layer of Earth below the crust (p. 20)

map: flat model of Earth's surface (p. 22)

map projection (proh-JEHK-shuhn): drawing of Earth's surface, or part of it, on a flat surface (p. 24)

mass: amount of matter in something (p. 4)

meniscus: curve at the surface of a liquid in a thin tube (p. 4)

meridian (muh-RIHD-ee-uhn): line on a map or globe running from the North Pole to the South Pole along Earth's surface (p. 26)

metamorphic (meht-uh-MAWR-fihk) **rock:** rock formed when existing rocks are changed by heat and pressure (p. 66)

meter: basic unit of length or distance (p. 4)

mineral (MIHN-uhr-uhl): naturally occurring, inorganic solid formed from elements or compounds and having a definite chemical makeup and a regular atomic structure (p. 46)

model: tool scientists use to represent an object or a process (p. 3)

mold: imprint or hollow in rock that is shaped like and made by an organism (p. 90)

molecule: (MAHL-ih-kyool): smallest part of a substance that has all the properties of that substance (p. 42)

molten (MOHL-tuhn) **rock:** melted minerals (p. 68)

nonclastic rock: sedimentary rock made up of dissolved minerals or the remains of living things (p. 74)

nonfoliated: texture of a metamorphic rock that does not have mineral crystals arranged in bands (p. 78)

ore: mineral that is mined because it contains useful metals or nonmetals (p. 58)

parallel (PAR-uh-lehl): horizontal line on a map or globe that circles Earth from east to west at intervals starting at the equator (p. 26)

physical property: observable characteristic that describes an object (p. 48)

pluton (PLOO-tahn): large body of igneous rock that can form into different shapes when magma cools inside Earth's crust (p. 68)

precipitation (pree-sihp-uh-TAY-shuhn): process that occurs when elements and compounds leave a solution and crystallize out as solids (p. 54)

relative (REHL-uh-tihv) **age:** age of an object compared to the age of another object (p. 96)

rock: mixture of minerals, generally cemented together (p. 66)

rock cycle: series of natural processes by which rocks are slowly changed from one kind of rock to another kind of rock (p. 80)

scale: feature that relates distances on a map to actual distances on Earth's surface (p. 28)

sediment (SEHD-uh-muhnt): rock particles carried and deposited by water, wind, or ice (p. 72)

sedimentary (sehd-uh-MEHN-tuhr-ee) **rock:** rock formed from pieces of other rocks that are pressed together (p. 66)

simulation: computer model that usually shows a process (p. 3)

solution: mixture in which the particles of one substance are evenly mixed with the particles of another substance (p. 54)

specialist (SPEHSH-uhl-ihst): person who studies or works on only one part of a subject (p. 16)

specialty: studying or working in only one part of a subject (p. 16)

sphere (SFEER): round, three-dimensional object (p. 18)

streak: color of the powder left by a mineral (p. 48)

subscript (SUHB-skrihpt): number in a chemical formula that shows how many of each atom are in one molecule of a compound (p. 44)

symbol: drawing on a map that represents a real object (p. 28)

temperature: measurement of the amount of heat energy something contains (p. 4)

texture (TEHKS-chuhr): size of crystals in an igneous rock (p. 70)

theory: set of hypotheses that have been supported by testing over and over again (p. 10)

topography (tuh-PAHG-ruh-fee): general form and shape of the land on Earth's surface (p. 32)

unit: amount used to measure something (p. 4)

variable: anything that can affect the outcome of an experiment (p. 11)

volume: amount of space an object takes up (p. 4)

Index

Photo Credits

Photography Credits: All photographs are by the Pearson Learning Group (PLG), John Serafin for PLG, and David Mager for PLG, except as noted below.

Cover: *bkgd.* Photo Researchers, Inc.; *inset* John Cancalosi/Peter Arnold, Inc.

Table of Contents: iv: b Charles D. Winters/Photo Researchers, Inc.; v: t Chromosohm/Photo Researchers, Inc.; v b Jeff J. Daly/Fundamental Photographs

Frontmatter: P001 bl Science VU/Visuals Unlimited, Inc.; P001 mr George Ranalli/Photo Researchers, Inc.; P001 tr Farrell Grehan/Photo Researchers, Inc.; P001 Comstock, Inc.; P002 bl Jane Grushow/Grant Heilman Photography, Inc.; P002 br Eric Kamp/Phototake; P002 tr AFP/Corbis; P003 Comstock, Inc.; P005 Pearson Learning; P005 r Comstock, Inc.; P007 r Comstock, Inc.; P009 br Bob Daemmrich/Stock, Boston, Inc.; P009 mr USDA/Natural Resources Conservation Service; P009 tr SuperStock, Inc.; P009 r Comstock, Inc.; P010 Frans Lanting/Minden Pictures; P011 r Comstock, Inc.; P013 r Comstock, Inc.

Chapter 1: P015 NASA/Science Photo Library/Photo Researchers, Inc.; P016 bl Bob Daemmrich/Stock, Boston, Inc.; P016 br Runk Schoenberger/Grant Heilman Photography, Inc.; P016 tl USDA/Natural Resources Conservation Service; P016 tr SuperStock, Inc.; P017 l Science VU/Visuals Unlimited, Inc.; P017 r Tom Bean/DRK Photo; P018 Kim Heacox/DRK Photo; P021 The Granger Collection; P022 l Jeff Greenberg/Omni-Photo Communications; P022 tr Ric Feld/AP/Wideworld Photos; P023 CNES; Licensed by SPOT Image Corporation/Photo Researchers, Inc.; P025 Hulton Archive/Archive Photos; P029 Anne Braggins; P030 b American Philosphical Society; P030 t E. R. Degginger/Color-Pic, Inc.; P031 bl Bettmann/Corbis; P031 br Bettmann/Corbis; P031 tl United States Mint; P031 tr LewisandClarktrail.com; P032 Maps a la carte, Inc. and TopoZone.com (www.topozone.com); P033 Mark Gibson/Visuals Unlimited, Inc.; P038 NASA/Science Photo Library/Photo Researchers, Inc.; P039 NASA/Science Photo Library/Photo Researchers, Inc.; P040 NASA/Science Photo Library/Photo Researchers, Inc.

Chapter 2: P041 Dennis Flaherty/Photo Researchers, Inc.; P042 l Runk Schoenberger/Grant Heilman Photography, Inc.; P042 r Dane S. Johnson/Visuals Unlimited, Inc.; P043 br Hulton/Getty Images; P043 tl Martyn F. Chillmaid/Science Photo Library/Photo Researchers, Inc.; P043 tr Lawrence Migdale/Photo Researchers, Inc.; P045 Charles D. Winters/Photo Researchers, Inc.; P046 Kent Foster/Photo Researchers, Inc.; P048 bc Harry Taylor/Dorling Kindersley Limited; P048 bl E. R. Degginger/Color-Pic, Inc.; P048 br Paul Silverman/Fundamental Photographs; P048 tr Fundamental Photographs; P050 b Gary Retherford/Photo Researchers, Inc.; P050 t Breck P. Kent/Animals Animals/Earth Scenes; P051 Gemaldegalerie, Dresden, Germany/Bridgeman Art Library; P051 inset Thessalonika Museum, Greece/Bridgeman Art Library; P052 b Charles D. Winters/Photo Researchers, Inc.; P052 t Colin Keates/Dorling Kindersley Limited; P053 Lawrence Stoller; P055 NASA; P055 inset NASA/Phototake; P058 bl Charles D. Winters/Photo Researchers, Inc.; P058 br M. Clayel Jacama/Photo Researchers, Inc.; P058 t Biophoto Associates/Photo Researchers, Inc.; P059 br Photo by Robert Weldon; P059 tl Hartmann/Sachs/Phototake; P059 tr Colin Keates/Dorling Kindersley Limited; P060 inset John Weinstein/The Field Museum of Natural History; P060-061 bkgd Peter Essick/Aurora & Quanta Productions; P061 b Smithsonian; P061 m Jerome Wexler/Visuals Unlimited, Inc.; P061 tl E. R. Degginger/Color-Pic, Inc.; P061 tm Richard M. Busch; P061 tr Natural History Museum/Dorling Kindersley Limited; P062 Dennis Flaherty/Photo Researchers, Inc.; P063 Dennis Flaherty/Photo Researchers, Inc.; P064 Dennis Flaherty/Photo Researchers, Inc.

Chapter 3: P065 Carr Clifton/Minden Pictures; P066 Chromosohm/Photo Researchers, Inc.; P067 Dr. Michael Howell; P068 Michael Nicholson/Corbis; P069 John Kay/Corbis; P070 l Phillip Hayson/Photo Researchers, Inc.; P070 r Breck P. Kent/Animals Animals/Earth Scenes; P073 b Ric Ergenbright/Corbis; P073 inset O.S.F./Animals Animals/Earth Scenes; P073 tl Colin Keates/Dorling Kindersley Limited; P073 tr Runk/Schoenberger/Grant Heilman Photography, Inc.; P074 b Farrell Grehan/Photo Researchers, Inc.; P074 m Andrew J. Martinez/Photo Researchers, Inc.; P074 t Joyce Photographics/Photo Researchers, Inc.; P076 bl Phillip Hayson/Photo Researchers, Inc.; P076 br Grace Davies/Omni-Photo Communications; P076 tl Phillip Hayson/Photo Researchers, Inc.; P076 tr Grace Davies/Omni-Photo Communications; P077 Paul Jenkin/Animals Animals/Earth Scenes; P078 bl Tom Pantages/Phototake; P078 br Andrew J. Martinez/Photo Researchers, Inc.; P078 tl Andrew J. Martinez/Photo Researchers, Inc.; P078 tr Andrew J. Martinez/Photo Researchers, Inc.; P079 b Malcolm S. Kirk/Peter Arnold, Inc.; P079 t Grace Davies/Omni-Photo Communications; P084 b Dennis Oda/Getty Images; P084 t Michael Nicholson/Corbis; P085 b Emma Lee/PhotoDisc, Inc.; P085 m Carr Clifton/Minden Pictures; P085 t Chris R. Sharp/Photo Researchers, Inc.; P086 Carr Clifton/Minden Pictures; P087 Carr Clifton/Minden Pictures; P088 Carr Clifton/Minden Pictures

Chapter 4: P089 John Cancalosi/Peter Arnold, Inc.; P090 l E. R. Degginger/Color-Pic, Inc.; P090 r Carolina Biological Supply/Phototake; P091 bl Tom McHugh/Photo Researchers, Inc.; P091 tl Jonathan Blair/Corbis; P091 tr Jeff J. Daly/Fundamental Photographs; P094 Tom McHugh/Photo Researchers, Inc.; P095 Des Bartlett/Photo Researchers, Inc.; P099 John Reader/Science Photo Library/Photo Researchers, Inc.; P101 Steve Munsinger/Photo Researchers, Inc.; P102 John Weinstein/The Field Museum of Natural History; P103 Glenn Short/Liaison Agency, Inc.; P106 John Cancalosi/Peter Arnold, Inc.; P107 John Cancalosi/Peter Arnold, Inc.; P108 John Cancalosi/Peter Arnold, Inc.